# WEALTH BUILDING

## IN THE

# 90ˢ

## WHAT WALL STREET WON'T TELL YOU!

# WEALTH BUILDING

## IN THE

# 90ˢ

## WHAT WALL STREET WON'T TELL YOU!

Michael L. Yergin, Laura A. Graves, and Robert G. Chenhall, Ph.D.

---

Chicago Financial Publications, Inc.
Chicago, Illinois

The opinions and recommendations presented in this book are based upon the authors' experience and should not be relied upon as an assurance or guaranty of profit. Moreover, while the authors believe the information disclosed herein to be accurate at the time of its writing, no guarantee of accuracy or completeness is made. The authors are involved directly in the rare coin market and may buy and sell coins consistently or inconsistently with the recommendations made herein due to the fact that the rare coin market changes on a daily basis.

Published by
Chicago Financial Publications, Inc.
500 North Michigan Avenue, Suite 1920
Chicago, Illinois 60611

Library of Congress Cataloging-in-Publication Data
Yergin, Michael L.
  Wealth Building in the 90s: What Wall Street Won't Tell You
  Includes index
    1. Coins as an Investment.   2. Investments
    I. Graves, Laura A. II. Chenhall, Ph.D., Robert G.   III. Title
Library of Congress Catalog Card Number 90-085044
ISBN 0-9627115-0-0

Printed and Manufactured in the United States of America

Book Design by Stuart J. Millman

First Printing
10  9  8  7  6  5  4  3  2  1

# ACKNOWLEDGMENTS

The hardest part of any book is always writing the acknowledgments. There are so many people who have put their blood, sweat, and tears into an endeavor such as this that the authors' biggest fear is always forgetting to mention someone. So, thank you to everyone involved in writing and gathering the material for this book.

Michael and Laura would like to thank Sonny Bloch for introducing his national audience of devoted listeners to the benefits of rare coin investing.

Thanks also go out to Bill Bresnan of New York's WABC Talk Radio for explaining to his listeners the merits of rare coin investing.

The authors are indebted to Dan Peterson of Chicago Financial Publications, Inc., to Maurice Rosenthal of Washington Communications and Publicity Corporation, our publicist in Washington, DC, who each helped bring this book to the public's eye and to Gerilee Hundt for her invaluable assistance.

We would also like to thank Arthur Yergin, Barbara Chenhall, Erv Beskow, the fine folks at the American Numismatic Association in Colorado, Luis Vigdor and Howard Segermark from ICTA, the Consumer Numismatic Advisory Commission, Ned Fenton from SafraBank (California), David Hall and his staff at the Professional Coin Grading Service, Duke Brodsky, Erin Langdon, Todd Haitz, Clyde Culen, James Barber, Shelley Stout, and Richard Davis.

We extend special thanks to Stuart J. Millman, our Macintosh®
computer guru, who worked relentlessly in handling rewrites and
layouts and who worked long hours in association with Chicago Financial Publications supervising the timely completion of this project.

Finally, we want to thank the person who has given us health, wis-
dom, and inspiration. God bless you all as much as he has blessed us.

*This book is dedicated to all of our
friends who have profited in the
rare coin market and to the
masses who haven't
… yet!*

# CONTENTS

# ILLUSTRATIONS

# FOREWORD

*Wealth Building in the 90s* is somewhat unique among the many books devoted to making money. It is a "how-to" book that shows you, step-by-step, how to create wealth with hard assets—specifically by investing in rare coins. It is written by knowledgeable, "insider" experts, and is a serious attempt to protect the rare coin investor, who usually is something less than an expert numismatist, by providing a level playing field for dealing with coin dealers and the rare coin limited partnerships now being sold by Wall Street brokerage firms.

This book probably will make some people in the industry very unhappy with its honesty, but it will show you, the investor, how to make a lot of money in rare coins—which I have been doing for many years.

The authors of *Wealth Building in the 90s* combine a wealth of knowledge in numismatics, finance, and investments. I happen to know the senior author, Michael Yergin, best. He is my hard money guru. My daily show is broadcast live to over 200 cities in the USA—our telephone lines are always open for questions from the listening public and we handle over 7,000 calls on the air each year. When my listeners have a question about rare coins, I call my expert, Mr. Yergin.

In his early twenties Michael had already become a millionaire by developing condominiums and by building and managing hotels in Chicago and Florida. In 1979 and 1980, he saw construction money go from 11% to 22%, and he lost millions. But at the same time his rare coins appreciated in value. Fortunately for us, he had the insight to see then what was on the financial horizon, and, as the saying goes, "the rest is history."

Michael is an authority on rare coins. He makes money for people, and through this "must read" book, he shares his secrets of success with you.

The advice provided in *Wealth Building in the 90s* will enable you to begin immediately to gain the large financial rewards that insiders have realized for years through rare coin investments.

—H.I. Sonny Bloch

Sonny Bloch has a nationally syndicated radio program on real estate investing that is heard on over 200 stations throughout the United States. His success as a real estate authority has been heralded in magazines such as *Money* and *Readers Digest*, and on national television. During one of his appearances on "Nightline," Ted Koppel said of him, "He talks to more people about real estate than anyone else in America." Mr. Bloch is the author of two best-selling books: *Inside Real Estate* and *171 Ways to Make Money in Real Estate*.

# Chapter 1

# WE ALL WANT TO BE RICH—THE NEW GUARANTEED WAY TO ACHIEVE IT

We all want to be rich—and now, long-untold secrets guarantee that you can attain the riches you want!

Question: What do Buddy Ebsen (better known as Barnaby Jones), Thomas Jefferson, Gary Burghoff (Radar O'Reilly on the hit TV series "M*A*S*H"), the opera singer Enrico Caruso, pianist Hoagie Carmichael, world famous violinist Jascha Heifetz, King Farouk of Egypt, hockey star Wayne Gretzky, Congressman Jimmy Hayes, King Gyges of Lydia (modern Turkey), the Rothschild Family, and Swiss bankers all have in common?

Answer: They all have increased their wealth by investing in rare coins. Many people, including some of those referred to above, have become millionaires this way.

Now you, too, can follow in the footsteps of those who have profited from coin investing. You can plot your own investment course by utilizing the information disclosed in this book. We will show you how to make money, lots of money, by following certain methods and using certain heretofore secret information to your advantage.

## SEVEN REASONS TO INVEST IN RARE COINS

Why in the world would you be interested in parking a portion of your hard-earned investment portfolio in rare coins? The answer is simple: to make more money than you can by parking it someplace else. According to a *Wall Street Journal* scoreboard comparing the total returns from a wide range of different investments (Figure 1), rare coins appreciated over 50% in 1989 alone.

But there are at least six other compelling reasons for investing in coins. Let's discuss all of them.

Reason #1—HIGH PROFITS

The only reason people make investments rather than leaving their money in the bank or under a mattress is to earn more money than a bank is willing to pay for the use of their funds.

When you consider any new form of investment, there are never absolute guarantees that it will be profitable, or if so, how profitable. But it is always helpful to find out how successful that type of investment has been in the past.

The history of the rare coin market demonstrates clearly that wise investments in coins over the last 40 years have outperformed all other nonleveraged investments. A study by David Hall, president of the Professional Coin Grading Service, compared the performance of gem-quality rare coins with the Consumer Price Index from 1950 to 1988 (Figure 2). The average compounded increase in value of the coins was *20.28% per year* over the *entire 38 years*.

Other studies, using different sources of information, have produced slightly different results (for example, the Salomon Brothers' 1988 survey reproduced here as Figure 3), but the comparative ranking of different investments always lead to conclusions similar to those on the Salomon Brothers' survey: "Compounded annual rates of return on coin investments have exceeded those of all other assets over both 20-year and 10-year periods."

In the 1970 to 1974 bull market, prices for top-quality coins increased between 200 and 500%. In the 1976 to 1980 bull market, prices went up between 500 and 1,000%. Between August 1982 and December 1985 the *average* price increase for rare coins graded Mint State-65 was 158.9%.

# A COMPARISON OF
# INVESTMENT RETURNS

| | 1989 | 1988 | 1987 |
|---|---|---|---|
| **Stocks*** | | | |
| Dow Jones Industrial Average (30 stocks) | 32.35%[1] | 16.58% | 5.74% |
| Standard & Poor's 500 Stock Index | 31.53[1] | 17.07 | 5.23 |
| Wilshire 5000 Stock Index | 29.15[1] | 17.92 | 2.27 |
| | | | |
| **Bonds*** | | | |
| Shearson Lehman Long Term Treasure Index | 18.85%[1] | 9.19% | -2.67% |
| Shearson Lehman Long Term AA-Rated Bond Index | 15.54[1] | 10.05 | -0.69 |
| Shearson Lehman Municipal Bond Index | 10.19[1] | 10.16 | 1.51 |
| Shearson Lehman Intermediate Term Treasury Index | 12.58[1] | 6.26 | 3.60 |
| Shearson Lehman Mortgage-Backed Securities Index | 15.40[1] | 8.72 | 4.28 |
| | | | |
| **Mutual Funds*** | | | |
| Lipper Growth Fund Index | 28.54%[1] | 15.78% | 1.02% |
| Lipper Growth and Income Fund Index | 21.63[1] | 19.47 | 3.15 |
| Lipper Balanced Fund Index | 20.85[1] | 7.86 | 2.03 |
| Lipper International Fund Index | 23.59[1] | 18.10 | 4.80 |
| | | | |
| **Bank Instruments*** | | | |
| (Bank Rate Monitor National Index) | | | |
| One-Year Certificate of Deposit | 8.67% | 7.66% | 6.92% |
| 30-Month Certificate of Deposit | 8.59 | 7.99 | 7.34 |
| Money Market Deposit Account | 6.46 | 5.86 | 5.60 |
| | | | |
| **Money Market Fund*** | | | |
| Donoghue's 12-month yield on all taxable money funds | 8.90%[1] | 7.11% | 6.12% |
| | | | |
| **Precious Metals** (bars of bullion) | | | |
| Platinum (50 oz) | -5.67% | 4.30% | 6.26% |
| Gold (100 oz ) | -1.83 | -15.24 | 20.98 |
| Silver (1,000 oz) | -13.63 | -10.15 | 23.02 |
| | | | |
| **Residential Real Estate** | | | |
| Increase in average price of new single-family home | 10.9% | 7.6% | 13.7% |
| | | | |
| **Collectibles** | | | |
| Sotheby's Old Master Paintings Index | 40.7%[2] | 25.7% | 23.1% |
| Rare Coins, top investment grade | 50.6[2] | 26.2 | 13.2 |
| (Coin World Trends survey) | | | |

*Includes reinvestment of dividends or interest, if any.  [1]estimate  [2]As of Nov. 30

Source: *Wall Street Journal* January 2, 1990

Figure 1

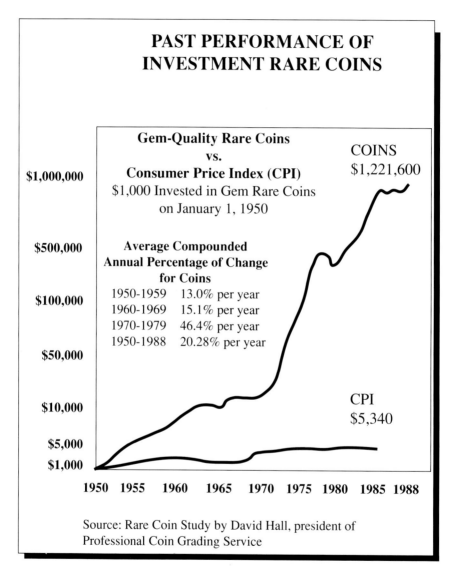

Figure 2

## COMPOUND ANNUAL RATES OF RETURN[1] COMPARING VARIOUS INVESTMENT VEHICLES

| Category | 20 yrs. | 10 yrs. | 5 yrs. | 1 yr. |
|---|---|---|---|---|
| Coins | 15.1% | 13.4% | 10.1% | 14.0% |
| U.S. Stamps | 12.9 | 10.5 | 0.2 | 1.4 |
| Gold | 12.8 | 9.6 | 2.2 | 3.1 |
| Chinese Ceramics | 12.0 | 9.2 | 5.5 | 10.5 |
| Oil | 9.9 | 3.7 | -10.7 | 19.5 |
| Diamonds | 9.9 | 9.6 | 7.5 | 24.9 |
| Old Masters | 8.8 | 8.8 | 12.0 | 13.4 |
| Treasury Bills | 8.5 | 10.1 | 7.6 | 6.0 |
| Bonds | 8.1 | 10.3 | 13.4 | 6.2 |
| Housing | 7.7 | 6.2 | 5.0 | 2.0 |
| Stocks | 6.8 | 13.3 | 13.8 | -4.9 |
| CPI | 6.3 | 6.1 | 3.3 | 3.1 |
| Silver | 5.9 | 2.8 | -11.6 | -7.4 |
| U.S. Farmland | 5.9 | 0.6 | -6.5 | 3.1 |
| Foreign Exchange | 4.7 | 3.2 | 9.5 | 8.5 |

[1]Returns are for the period ending June 1, 1988
Source: Salomon Brothers, Inc.

Figure 3

A $5,000 investment in quality rare coins on January 1, 1989, would have been worth $7,500 after only one year, and some coins appreciated in value as much as 250 percent in 1989. So, before you say, "It can never happen to me," consider these facts and think about some of the things you have always wanted to do: buy a new home, quit your job, open your own business. It is true that money will not buy happiness, but having money is certainly a lot better than not having it.

The bottom line is profits. And a bottom line fact is that rare coins are one of the most extraordinary profit-making investments anywhere. Over a period of four decades, they have outperformed all other investments, including stocks, bonds, real estate, diamonds, and works of art.

Everyone now knows that Wall Street is investing hundreds of millions of dollars in rare coin funds. For reasons we will show you, this cannot help but drive prices even higher. We are convinced that the prices of investment-grade high-quality coins will increase from 600 to 3,000% before the end of this decade.

With this book, you will learn how to take advantage of this situation, whether you have $500 or $500,000 to invest.

Reason #2—LIQUIDITY

Rare coins are the most liquid of all collectibles. A rare painting, for example, may retain its value, but it could take months or years for an investor to liquidate such a painting and realize a profit. Not so with coins.

The *Coin Dealer Newsletter* has published weekly dealer-to-dealer pricing information for all important U.S. coins since 1963. No other collectible has as frequently published a pricing structure. Two or three times a month there are major coin shows and coin auctions where your representative can sell your coins.

Thirty-one of the top coin dealers formed a market-making network in 1986 to dramatically increase liquidity for coin buyers and sellers. We suggest that you invest only in "certified" coins (we'll define this for you when we get into coin grading). One of the major reasons for suggesting this is because certified coins are traded on an exchange like shares of stock. What this means to the investor is that you may sell your coins at any time and receive your money immediately.

In addition, many dealer firms can put you in touch with several banks that offer asset-based loans on rare coins. The bank will hold your coins as collateral and lend you money against them, often on very short notice. As a result of lending policies such as this, you do not have to sell your coins if the market conditions are not right, but you can borrow against them.

Reason #3—DIMINISHING SUPPLY

Rare coins are unique in that the continually diminishing supply offers a very important investment advantage. They are not making any more $20 St. Gaudens or Buffalo Nickels or Walking Liberty Halves or Morgan Silver Dollars. Furthermore, the existing supply of previously minted U.S. coins is constantly diminishing due to melting, abuse, neglect, etc.

This is in sharp contrast to other investments. In the stock market, when a company needs more equity funding, it sells additional shares of stock, diluting the value of prior shareholders' investments. Those who invest in natural resources, such as oil, natural gas, gold, silver, and precious stones, likewise have to contend with constant price fluctuations due to the political control of production—for example, by the Organization of Petroleum Exporting Countries (OPEC). And even investments in securities such as Treasury bills, certificates of deposit, and so on suffer from an elastic supply. Because the government prints more money every day the value of financial instruments is consistently diluted by inflation.

The advantage of the constantly diminishing supply of coins is twofold:

First, any increase in demand makes price increases inevitable. The supply of coins cannot be increased; the only way any new demand can be satisfied is with higher prices.

And, second, a limited supply reduces the downside risk. When prices come down, they are not further depressed or hindered in their recovery by excess production the way prices are in the oil market. In fact, in the rare coin market, lower prices tend to drive coins off the market. Coin owners simply won't sell at the lower prices and do not offer what they have for sale unless they get nervous. This eventually causes the prices to rise again. Rare coin investments, therefore, have limited downside risk.

Will Rogers once said about real estate, "They simply ain't making it any more." The same thing is true about rare coins. The supply is diminishing daily and this adds up to an opportunity to make huge profits. It does not require a course in economics to understand supply and demand. Whenever there is an increased demand for something coupled with a diminishing supply, the prices can move only one direction, and that direction is up. This translates into big money for the rare coin investor who invests before Wall Street has an opportunity to corner the market.

Reason #4—AFFORDABILITY

A single fine art painting can cost a million dollars or more. The record now is approaching $100 million. Only a few exceptionally rare coins, on the other hand, cost more than $100,000. A new record high of $2.9 million for a set of coins was received at auction in May 1990, and just recently a super High-Relief 1907 St. Gaudens $20 gold piece, in Proof-68 condition, sold for $1.5 million. Top-of-the-line coins can be expensive, but the majority of coins we recommend range in price between $1,000 and $20,000.

The difference is that investment quality art, diamonds, and real estate all demand very large amounts of money for the purchase of a single item, whereas it is possible to buy important top-quality invest-ment coins for as little as $500. Thus, even those who have limited investment dollars can get started in coin investing.

Reason #5—TAX BENEFITS

This is seldom talked about but there are several significant tax advantages offered by rare coin investments.

First, you do not have to pay any income taxes on interest or dividends since there are none. In fact, no taxes whatsoever are due until you actually receive profits from selling your coins. For example, if you had purchased 20 silver dollars, minted in San Francisco and graded MS-65, for $10 each in 1977, and you still had them today, they would be worth over $5,000. Your profit on that $200 investment would be huge. So, how much income tax would you owe? None! You haven't sold the coins yet. You could even take them to the bank and borrow

$3,000 or more, using the coins as collateral, and possibly deduct the interest expense from your current tax bill.

One of the great advantages of having an Individual Retirement Account (IRA) is the fact that the earnings in an IRA produce a compounded, tax-free return that is considerably higher than a comparable personal investment in taxable stocks and bonds. The same compounding principle applies when your entire return is from asset appreciation—as it is with rare coins—rather than having a large portion of the return received in the form of taxable dividends or interest.

Even when coins are sold out of your portfolio, there is a measure of flexibility concerning when the gains and losses are reported for tax purposes. Dealers do not submit 1099 forms to the Internal Revenue Service on individual sales, as brokerage firms are required to do on each stock or bond transaction. This gives you a number of options that are not available when investing in other types of assets. For example, you often are able to treat a simultaneous sale and purchase of coins as a tax-free exchange.

Section 6045 of the Internal Revenue Code defines—though not very clearly—what are called "broker reporting requirements." The passage of the Tax Equity and Fiscal Responsibility Act (TEFRA) in 1981 gave the IRS a new mandate to make such reporting apply to many commodity transactions, a requirement that some IRS personnel interpreted to include coins.

The initial proposal by the IRS defined a "broker" as a person willing to transfer property, redeem securities, retrieve indebtedness, or engage in a transaction "... in securities, commodities or forward contracts for others." This regulation applied only to property regulated by the Commodity Futures Trading Commission (CFTC), plus certain other specific items.

Political controversy has surrounded this issue for nearly five years. A new proposed IRS regulation makes it clear that all gold and silver coins are intended to be reportable unless they are "numismatic items," which are defined as having a price of more than 15% above bullion content. Another way this exception has been defined is that a "numismatic item" is the coin itself rather than an investment primarily for the metal content of the coin.

The Industry Council for Tangible Assets is mounting a major effort to force clarification of the entire Section 6045 tax code provision, with the express intention of making explicit that *rare* coins, by definition, are *not* covered. This would not change the present reporting practices of the industry but it would take away from the IRS, presumably into perpetuity, the claim of some agents that rare coin transactions should be reported.

Reason #6—ANONYMITY

All of us have different degrees of confidence or paranoia about our federal bureaucracy. The government's increasing intrusion into the private affairs of United States citizens has become a major concern for all investors.

At the present time, neither investors in rare coins nor dealers handling rare coin transactions are required to provide any reports to the government. Thus, you can remain anonymous as a rare coin investor. In fact, many dealer firms assign a number to each account and deal with their clients entirely by number, refusing any request to reveal the owner of an account under any circumstances.

It should be pointed out that coins are not registered or assigned to anyone. They may be transferred from person to person or given away as gifts. Whoever holds a certified coin is free to dispose of it in any manner desired.

Reason #7—SECURITY

With the advent of standardized grading and associated encapsulation of coins by independent authenticating and grading services in 1986, persons who are not expert numismatists are assured that the certified coins they purchase are actually what they are claimed to be, accurately graded and genuine, and that the grades assigned and recorded in the slabs with the coins have been determined properly and without prejudice. The two major grading services, Professional Coin Grading Service and Numismatic Guaranty Corporation of America, guarantee to pay full market value for a coin if it turns out that it was, in fact, over-graded.

Moreover, the grades of certified coins do not change over time, and they are not dependent upon the subjective evaluation of any individual who may be examining them in the future. This has made rare coins one of the safest investments available to the general public.

## THE GOAL OF INVESTING—FINANCIAL SUCCESS

This is your blueprint for making money. We will share the secrets and give you the background to make a great deal of money. If our advice is followed you will win, and win big. It has taken us over thirty years watching the evolution of the coin market to gather the knowledge that others have tried to keep hidden. Now, in a few hours, you will have the information the "insiders" have kept secret for so long. Nothing is left out.

If you have read this far, you are already a winner because you haven't closed your mind to building wealth. Many people, for reasons as diverse as low self-esteem, fear of success, conditioning of their parents, etc., do have a real fear of being successful.

Maxwell Maltz, a famous plastic surgeon, in his best-selling book, *Psychocybernetics*, talks about people who come to him because they see a flaw in their physical appearance that they want changed so they can be beautiful. The interesting thing that Maltz reports is that after a completely successful plastic surgery operation, when many of these people look in a mirror, they still see themselves as unattractive. They are so used to envisioning themselves in a certain way that they cannot change what their eyes actually see.

Similarly, many people who have made or are just starting to make potential fortunes in high-quality rare coins still don't see themselves as successful investors. Even though they are making lots of money, they are not used to it. Recently, a coin dealer helped one couple make over $80,000 in just 31 days on an investment of $25,000. They could have made a great deal more with a little patience, but they couldn't sleep at night and sold out at that point because it was beyond their comfort level. They were not used to financial success and preferred to play it safe. This is not an uncommon experience in the dynamic rare coin market.

You should recognize that this book quite possibly will change your life, for it will make it possible for you to be financially successful. Those of you who can handle financial success will love what happens and will be able to enjoy the good life instead of just dreaming about it. If, however, you cannot imagine yourself being part of the good life, you had better change your thinking right now. If you can't, you will at least learn why *others* are able to live so well.

We mentioned that we expect top-quality rare coin prices to increase between 600 and 3,000 percent over the next few years. It is important that you understand the reasons for this. You will learn later in the book that Wall Street is pouring hundreds of millions of dollars into rare coin funds. And major corporations such as General Electric are buying entire rare coin companies. The handwriting is on the wall.

With all investments, timing is critical. For reasons that will be explained thoroughly, the time to get started in building your rare coin portfolio is *today*. The time to make big money in rare coins is *now*. And by big money we are not talking about 20–30% annual returns. Big money means *big* money.

This book will serve as your reference manual on the subject. After you have read it, you will find that you go back to it again and again. It does not describe some gimmick or get-rich-quick scheme but it is a complete guide to how the game really works. We have already discussed the big profits that you can expect to earn. In the chapters that follow you will find all of the essential information that you must have in order to realize those profits.

We do not advocate placing all of your investment dollars in any one investment—stocks, money market funds, *or* rare coins—but we do strongly recommend that rare coins should make up a good 15–20% of the average investor's portfolio.

## THE ROMANCE OF COINS

United States coins are intriguing, fascinating, and historic. This is why millions of Americans collect them today and why you as an investor will have someone to sell them to, the future collectors.

Be careful. Many investors are so fascinated with their first purchases they soon become avid collectors. We know one person who, upon returning from the post office, was so enthralled opening his purchase and looking at his coins that he almost had a serious auto accident.

Coin collecting became a rage in the 1850s in the United States and has grown ever since. Prior to that it was just the exportation of early U.S. coins for commerce and European collectors that preserved our early coinage. If it wasn't for these European collectors some of the finest known specimens of our early coinage would be lost to us now.

There are many fascinating coins and stories and it is this that fuels the continuing growth of collectors and investors. The following are just two examples dealing with the same coin.

The nickel that had to be redesigned: In 1883, the Mint released a new nickel, the Liberty Head type, or, as it is more commonly known, the "V" nickel, designed by Charles E. Barber. The first nickels released had Lady Liberty's head facing left on the obverse, surrounded by 13 stars and with the date below the head. The coin was unmilled on the edges. The reverse had "United States of America" around the periphery and "E PLURIBUS UNUM" at the base. The central design was a large Roman numeral five, or "V," surrounded by an open wreath. This design unfortunately presented an opportunity for some unscrupulous people, who gold-plated the nickels, crudely milled the edges, and passed them off on the unwary as $5 gold pieces. Thus, a 5¢ purchase could net $4.95 in change. A tidy profit for a nickel and a little effort! The nickel was redesigned shortly thereafter and the word "CENTS" replaced the motto "E PLURIBUS UNUM."

The Liberty Nickel series had yet another and more famous surprise in store for us. The series supposedly ended in 1912, followed by the Buffalo Nickel series in 1913. However, around 1920 a small ad was placed in the *Numismatist* magazine that offered to buy 1913 Liberty Nickels. There were no records of 1913 Liberty coinage or listing of dies in the Mint records for such a coin. The ad was placed by Samuel W. Brown, who ironically was assistant curator of the Mint from 1904 to 1907 and clerk at the Mint at the time the coins were struck. After the ads were run for several months, with buying offers raised from $500 to $600 for a single specimen, Brown showed up at the 1920 ANA show with five 1913 Liberty Nickels. Draw your own conclusions. The five pieces eventually passed into the hands of Colonel E.H. Green, son of the eccentric millionaire Hetty Green. Then, the pieces subsequently passed on to other owners including King Farouk who owned two different specimens. They have become very famous and now are valued in the price range of $1 million each.

In this book we concentrate on the financial aspects of rare coins, and on giving you the information needed to be a wise rare coin investor. However, there is a true romance to buying, selling, and owning coins. We can think of no other way that a person can have so much fun and make a lot of money in the process.

# Chapter 2

# OPPORTUNITIES FOR RARE COIN INVESTORS

## ASTOUNDING PRICE PERFORMANCE

As we have shown in the last chapter, properly selected rare coins in 1989 surpassed all other types of investments with a total return of over 50%. The returns from any investment vary from one year to another, of course, but the long-term record of coin investment has also been at or near the top of the scoreboard over 10 years, 20 years and 40 years.

Anne Kates (in *USA Today*, June 7, 1988) drew the following conclusions from the Salomon Brothers' survey (Figure 3):

"Rare coins have appreciated the most since 1968...Over the same 20-year stretch, stocks have barely beat inflation.

"Salomon's annual study pits financial mainstays such as stocks and bonds against other assets ranging from real estate to Chinese ceramics.

"The results (of this survey) show that if you invested $1,000 in rare coins in 1968, you'd have had $16,650 by June 1 (1988). Compare a $1,000 investment in stocks, reinvesting the dividends: You'd now have $3,727. The total return on high-grade corporate bonds—counting yields and price fluctuations—would have increased your $1,000 to $4,748."

These several studies are based upon different information sources, but the conclusion in every case is the same:

*High-quality rare coins are an excellent investment.*

Does everyone who owns coins realize a better return than provided by other investments? The answer, of course, is an unqualified "no." But, investors who have purchased the highest quality United States coins they could afford and have had the patience to hold onto their coins until market prices dictated that it was time to sell, have always, without exception, seen their wealth grow rapidly over the years. Many investors and collectors have become extremely wealthy buying and selling rare coins.

It is interesting to examine the differences between an investor and a collector. Most people probably look upon coin collectors as hobbyists who invest a great deal of time and money acquiring a particular series of "old coins." We cannot quite understand how they can receive any great artistic or other pleasure from just looking at or owning coins. However, we tolerate them as being harmless eccentrics.

But this is not the real story at all. Collectors have fostered their images as eccentric hobbyists in order to prevent the public from knowing about their real objective, which is and has always been to amass wealth! For decades, coin collectors have made incredible profits with their collections, but they would rather keep the secret to themselves than destroy it by too much publicity.

## WALL STREET ENTERS THE COIN MARKET

It is almost a truism that whenever large amounts of money are needed to finance potentially profitable endeavors, the investment bankers on Wall Street will find a way to put the project together—for a substantial fee, of course. Wall Street's entry into the coin market was exciting news, and a sure indication that a great deal of money could be made there in coming years.

Today, Wall Street is investing *heavily* in rare coins, not just bullion coins, which they have been buying and selling for a long time.

Bullion coins are neither rare nor old. Rather, they are modern-day, attractive gold, silver, and platinum coins, produced in quantity by a number of countries around the world. The primary purpose for minting bullion coins is to sell them to collectors or as gifts. Examples of bullion coins that are kept in inventory by one of the large brokerage firms include:

U.S. gold Eagle
U.S. silver Eagle
Canadian gold Maple Leaf
Australian Kangaroo Nugget
Australian platinum Koala
Mexican 50-Peso

We do not recommend that an investor ever buy bullion coins. There is too much risk. If gold and silver go up you make money; if they go down you lose. In other words, bullion coins are for amateur collectors, not the collectors we have talked about above, and they certainly are not appropriate for serious coin investors.

The price of a truly rare United States gold coin, weighing less than one ounce, often will continue to rise even when the prices of gold bullion and bullion coins are falling. Because the price of a rare gold coin is not tied to the gold market, gold could drop $200 an ounce and it would not affect the gold coin at all.

The involvement of the Wall Street firms in rare coin investments is something quite different from their handling of bullion coins as a product to buy and sell for their customers.

In addition to buying and selling securities—and bullion coins— brokerage firms have for many years been the primary organizers of limited partnerships. This is a unique form of organization in which the sponsoring institution serves as the general partner, responsible for all business activities of the partnership, and the limited partners are investors who buy "partnership interests" that are in many ways similar to the stock shares of publicly held corporations, although one such partnership interest usually is a great deal more expensive than a single share of stock.

The word "limited" is used to indicate that limited partners do not have the normal, "unlimited" liability for the debts of the partnership. In other words, they cannot lose more than their initial investments. Limited partnerships must be approved by the Securities and Exchange

Commission (SEC) before they can be offered to the public.

A limited partnership is most often the type of organization used to sponsor and finance a project that has a planned termination date, as opposed to an ongoing business venture, which, presumably, will continue into perpetuity. Limited partnerships often are formed to finance activities such as the building and eventual sale of a shopping center, the drilling of an oil well or a series of oil wells in a particular field, and so on.

The first rare coin limited partnership was initiated in 1979 by New England Rare Coin Galleries, headquartered in Boston. It was not until after the Professional Coin Grading Service (PCGS) was begun in 1986 that the big Wall Street investment firms began offering rare coin limited partnerships. Since then, almost all of the large Wall Street brokerage firms (and a number of others as well) have offered funds that plan to buy large inventories of coins and hold them for five or more years before selling the coins and liquidating the funds.

Merrill Lynch, Kidder Peabody, Shearson Lehman Hutton, and others all have set up funds for this purpose. The impact this will have on the coin market can be illustrated by what Kidder has done.

We must remember that Kidder Peabody is now owned by General Electric, which has also purchased one of the largest coin dealers in the business, James U. Blanchard and Company. Kidder Peabody also has an arrangement with two West Coast coin dealers, Hugh J. Scoyners and Kevin Lipton, and has organized KP Futures Management Corporation, with Scoyners as owner, for the purpose of buying and selling coins for their fund.

The initial offering by Kidder Peabody was scheduled to close to investors on March 31, 1989, after raising between $25 million and $40 million. A potential investor in the fund was required to start with a minimum of a $50,000 partnership interest. In the prospectus the financial qualifications of potential investors were stated as (1) a net worth of one million dollars, exclusive of cars and homes, and (2) an annual income of $200,000 for at least the last two years and an anticipated income of a like amount for the current year. This was obviously not intended to be a fund for the small investor. The fund is scheduled to be liquidated between the end of 1993 and the end of 1995, depending upon when the managers can receive the best prices in the

# Chapter **3**

# DO YOU NEED A COIN DEALER *OR* WALL STREET?

## THE FOUR WAYS AN INDIVIDUAL CAN BUY AND SELL COINS

In this chapter we will discuss the four basic methods by which a person can enter the coin market, and explain which is best to maximize your earnings. These are not entirely exclusive of one another—you can use one method one time and another at a different time—but it helps to separate the four so that the wise investor will learn the advantages and risks involved with each. The four approaches are:

-Attend shows and auctions yourself, and look through the inventories of small stamp and coin shops searching for unrecognized values;

-Buy from major coin dealers, either in person, if they have showrooms that are convenient, or by telephone ordering of "sight-unseen" coins for delivery by the U.S. Postal Service or Federal Express;

-Place your available funds in a managed account with a single dealer who will make all buy and sell decisions for you and charge you an annual fee for servicing the account and for storage and insurance of your coins; and

-Place your available funds in one or another of the limited partnerships that Wall Street offers.

It is fun to go to coin shows and auctions, to look at the coins on display and to talk to dealers and other collectors. Many of today's major dealers began their careers, often as teenagers, by joining coin clubs, and by buying, selling, and trading at local shows. As long as one does not have too much money to spend this can be an excellent way to learn the insider's point of view about the rare coin market and to observe both the "good deals" that occasionally occur and the "bad deals," which often result in the unwary buyer becoming a victim. In addition, when you are trading with the part-time dealers who travel from one show to another, you occasionally can make purchases for less than the normal dealer markup. It can be a good learning experience for anyone who is serious about the coin market.

That is the good side of buying coins yourself. However, there are many negative aspects to this kind of trading as well. You absolutely must either buy nothing but "slabbed" coins, which are guaranteed to be authentic and properly graded, or you must have the skills of an expert numismatist to be able to authenticate and accurately grade coins yourself. We cannot emphasize this too strongly, no matter what method is used to acquire rare coins.

The most common mistakes made by beginning coin investors are 1) thinking they know more than they really do about numismatics, and 2) accepting uncritically what they are told by an unknown dealer about the condition, grade, and prices of coins they purchase. Even experienced traders sometimes have trouble picking up the minor marks that identify a coin as a fake, as having been altered, or as properly graded two or three levels below what the seller is claiming. For the novice, a mistake like this can mean paying thousands of dollars more than the true market value for a coin. We want to be sure you do not make this mistake.

In future chapters, we will show you how coins are graded, how to determine rarity, and how to decide the reasonableness of prices. These are all things you should know in order to invest wisely. But, fortunately, the investor today does not have to acquire the skills of a professional coin grader. We suggest that you *always* buy coins that have been authenticated, graded, and placed in tamperproof plastic slabs by either the Professional Coin Grading Service (PCGS) or the Numismatic Guaranty Corporation of America (NGC), and not depend upon your own knowledge for this purpose. Since 1986, the grading services have made it unnecessary for you to become a grader yourself in order to be a successful coin investor.

You will find that at coin shows even accurately graded coins often are priced higher than what the seller really expects to receive. You never know when someone unskilled in these matters will come along and pay what you are asking. Besides, you can always come down in price if confronted by a serious and knowledgeable buyer. The bid and ask prices on rare coins are seldom etched in stone. Prices more often are set to allow for some bargaining. But, you must decide the maximum price that you are willing to pay, and stick to it! Learn to buy intelligently, not emotionally. Don't get caught up in your desire to own "that" coin. Stay cool, level headed, as though you have been doing this sort of thing all your life. Always wear a poker face when you are negotiating to buy or sell.

Coin auctions involve everything that is said above about coin shows plus a special factor that can only be described as the emotion of the moment and the seriousness of any individual to obtain a particular coin "no matter what."

There are many skills in proper auction buying and that perhaps is the reason why buying at auctions is best left to a professional bidder.

First and foremost is preparation. You must view the lots in advance, do your research, set maximum bids and *stick to them.* Having an auction catalogue clearly marked by circling the lot numbers you plan to bid on and marking your maximum bids down in code will greatly help, as you don't want your competitors to look over your shoulder and see your maximum bid.

Auction lots go off at one to three per minute. Thus, this is not the time to be calculating your bids. Knowing your maximum will keep you from getting caught up in auction fever and paying too much for your selected lots. Mark your catalogue with opening bids, closing bids, and the successful bidder's number. This can give you market information on what coins are going for and who is buying them.

Know the increments an auctioneer uses based on the dollar value of the item being auctioned. The tempo of the auction is very important.

Knowing the increments of the bidding and selecting the proper time to get your bid recognized will allow you to be at your maximum bid as bidding goes back and forth between you and your competitors. For example, if your maximum bid is $300 for an item and the bidding increments are at $25, you don't want to jump in at $275. Your competition will get recognized at $300, your top price. Now you must drop out or exceed your maximum. Instead, jump in at $250. Your competition bids $275 and your maximum bid of $300 will be recognized. In a large auction this can secure a larger portion of your desired items and save you from having to exceed your limits to secure your lots. Of course, sometimes bids exceed your maximums no matter what your preparation is. Let them go!

Selecting a seat where you have a full view of the auctioneer and he can see you clearly is very important. You don't want to have to furiously wave your paddle or yell out to get the auctioneer's attention. Remember, you are going to have to jump into the auction at precise times. Auctioneers are professionals too and they learn who is bidding on certain material. An auctioneer's eyes will automatically move toward you, and if you are seated properly, he will notice your intent to bid. You also may not wish your competitors to know you are bidding. If properly seated, a subtle motion with a pen or a nod will be recognized by the auctioneer. Don't develop too many different signs, though. Most auctioneers aren't *that* good. Stick with a few basic signals or you might buy something while stretching!

There are of course many more things one can learn, but experience is perhaps one of the best teachers. Hopefully, these few tips will be of help to you or help you decide to have an expert do your auction bidding. There are additional advantages in having a dealer represent you at an auction. For instance, for a variety of reasons you may wish to buy or sell coins while remaining anonymous. Purchases for your account, either by auction or at coin conventions, can be made without revealing that they are being made on your behalf. Moreover, a dealer can almost always buy cheaper and, even if adding a modest commission, save you money. A dealer with good contacts and resources has the time to devote to digging out the best scarce and rare coins and can often get you material you would never find.

In May 1990 a coin auction at Superior Stamp and Coin in Beverly

Hills drew many entertainment and sports personalities. One of these was ice hockey star Wayne Gretzky, bidding for his own account. He purchased the Hamilton Fish Family 1873 Pattern Trade Dollar Presentation Set for $125,000, plus the 10% buyer's commission. Mr. Gretzky undoubtedly wanted this set as a collector. Just think what will happen when other celebrities start buying, along with Wall Street. The public then will flock into the market like sheep and pay prices that are in line with where you want to sell.

Immediately following the Gretzky purchase, the world-famous "King of Siam" set was sold to a dealer, Iraj Sayah. He paid a record $2,900,000 for the set, in addition to the 10% "buyer's fee" that went to the auction house. Sixty seconds was all it took for numismatic history to be made. The set was bought in the name of Sayah's company, Unigold, and an anonymous, "collector" partner.

Auctions are emotionally exciting and they can be very educational. In addition, the careful buyer can sometimes find real bargains this way. But the wise investor will always know in advance the maximum prices he is willing to pay, and he will maintain sufficient control over the situation not to bid much more than his predetermined maximum price for any coin.

Another way to buy coins is from major coin dealers. These dealers may be located anywhere. They advertise widely and most often the initial contact is the result of an interested buyer either answering a magazine advertisement or responding to a radio solicitation with a telephone call. Many reputable dealers do virtually all of their business by mail and phone, and they provide investors with full value for their money. However, there are also many coin dealer firms that can best be called telemarketing "bucket shops."

*Always* make certain you are dealing with a company that sells only PCGS and NGC-certified coins. This allows the salespeople to state with honesty that the authenticity and grading of their coins is guaranteed. Perhaps it isn't necessary to repeat the obvious, but a person should never, under any circumstances, buy coins that are *not* PCGS or NGC-graded without being able to physically examine the coins before the sale is finalized. In other words, do not buy unslabbed coins from any dealer based upon a salesperson's telephone call. And do not send money for any coin purchase on the basis of a verbal money-back guarantee.

It is normal for a dealer firm to protect itself against customer dishonesty by requiring that funds for all purchases be in their hands before coins are shipped to you. This is accomplished either by a bank wire of the funds or by holding the delivery of your coins until your check has been cleared, which normally takes less than a week even if it is from out of state. However, when buying from any dealer the first time, wait until your coins are delivered before placing a second order so you will have some idea of that company's customary shipping procedures. Shipment should take place shortly after your check has cleared the bank if the coin is in the dealer's inventory. If the coin has to be acquired for you on the wholesale market delivery could take a little longer.

From the paragraphs above, and what we present in the chapter on pricing (Chapter 6), it should be apparent why the next section on "Selecting the Right Dealer" *must* be read before your make your first purchase.

A third method of buying and selling coins is to place the money you have allocated to this type of investment in the hands of a reliable dealer, with authorization to buy and sell for your account without contacting you in advance and without shipping the coins to you for storage. This is commonly referred to as a "managed account," and it works, with minor exceptions, the same way that a managed securities account is handled.

In a managed securities account, the advisor who determines what is to be bought and sold may be an employee of the brokerage firm with whom orders are placed but usually the account advisor and the account broker are independent companies. With managed coin accounts the advisor and the dealer are most often the same firm. In both kinds of accounts, minimum balances—usually from $10,000 to as much as $500,000 or more—are required in order to establish the account, and fees are charged for the management. With managed coin accounts, the management fee may be as low as 1% of the principal value per year, plus a similar charge for storage and insurance.

Managed accounts can produce the best overall return of any kind of coin investment *if* the account manager is capable and conscientious about buying and selling at the most favorable prices. The investor does not have to have any knowledge about coins in order to produce a good return on his investment. He simply invests his money with a dealer and allows the dealer to buy and sell whatever coins he or she considers appropriate. However, even though you do not know in advance what is going to happen in your account, you should always be kept informed by written confirmations covering each transaction. And should your financial position change at any time, a conscientious dealer will accommodate your wishes by taking steps to help you borrow against the account at a bank that provides loans on rare coins, or by selling some of the collection or, if necessary, liquidating the account.

An investment in PCGS and NGC-certified rare coins has the complete liquidity of, say, a money market fund or ownership of individual stocks and bonds. Stocks usually can be sold in a day or less, with settlement one week later. A managed coin account may settle just as fast, but to maximize your profits it is often in your best interest to allow enough time for the dealer to sell your coins, perhaps on a consignment basis, to another interested investor. This may take a little more time.

Finally, there is a fourth method of investing in coins: place the money you have allocated to this investment in the hands of your stock broker to purchase for your account as many limited partnership interests as the money will buy. This method of investing also has the advantage of not requiring any further management or direct participation by the investor. Once you make the decision to buy into the limited partnership you can sit back and wait for the managers of the fund to carry out the original plan in, say, five years or more.

Prior to the 1986 Tax Reform Act limited partnerships provided an excellent investment for wealthy persons because the investor's proportionate share of partnership losses could be offset against other earned income during the life of the partnership, with the gains at the end of the venture (usually when the assets of the partnership were sold) taxed at capital gains rates. Today, the losses can only be offset against "passive income," earned from other similar ventures and, of course, there is no longer any tax advantage to "long-term capital gains." Nevertheless, if a person has unused passive losses from other limited partnerships—losses which otherwise would not be deductible—a profitable limited partnership produces the equivalent of nontaxable income.

While investing in a coin limited partnership may be well suited to a particular investor, and it may produce a good financial return, we believe that most coin investors do not need Wall Street. You can make a great deal more money by investing in rare coins directly, for your own account, and controlling your own financial destiny.

Keep in mind when selecting one of the alternatives as an entrance into the coin market that each method has certain advantages. When you take physical possession of coins or purchase them via a managed account, you preserve the tax advantages of rare coin investing. You also have liquidity. When investing in a limited partnership you do not have liquidity and only in special situations is there any tax advantage. Also, you are required to report all transactions and your proportionate part of the partnership gain or loss.

It is perhaps obvious that each of these four ways of trading coins meets the financial and aesthetic or emotional needs of some group of collectors/investors. If it did not it would cease to exist. However, the *best* way for you to build wealth in the nineties is to take that first step now and start buying coins for your own portfolio. How you choose to buy is a matter for you to decide, and the amount of money put into the market is not important. But *timing is critical.*

The Wall Street funds are buying heavily now. Once the investing public becomes aware of what they have been missing, they will undoubtedly create a rare coin investment craze. The inevitable result will be an excess of investment funds attempting to buy a limited quantity of rare coins. When this occurs, prices *always* rise to unreasonable heights. By the time investor euphoria sets in, the major profits will already have been made—by those who begin now!

## SELECTING THE RIGHT DEALER

Anyone investing in rare coins sooner or later finds it necessary to do business with a coin dealer; and the first lesson to making money in rare coins is to find a dealer whom you trust and can work with comfortably. No matter how knowledgeable you become in the field of numismatics, you will find that a good dealer always knows more and has more contacts than you do.

The second lesson to learn in order to make money with coins is to buy only from dealers whose credentials are known to you. Make the effort; take the time to check out any dealer you think you are going to start working with. Do not buy from dealers who are unknown to you. The result is almost always less than satisfactory, in one way or another, and it usually results in your spending more money than you need to for the coins you acquire.

Since the American Numismatic Exchange came into being, wise investors (through their dealers) can know exactly what the lowest asking price is on any coin and who their dealer should contact in order to buy that coin. This information is also available from the Certified Coin Exchange (CCE), which is another network for trading PCGS and NGC-certified coins. Although the asking price has a profit built in and your dealer will also have to add a markup in order to stay in business, pricing is no longer "what the market will bear," with "the market" being the potential buyer facing the dealer at the moment. This system now in operation has cut into dealers' margins and put many coin shops out of business. But it also has produced a marketplace in which honest, well-financed dealers can serve their clients well. A well-versed dealer will have bids placed on the ANE or CCE systems and can charge you a commission based on his bids, and not on the ask price, and thus save you considerable dollars.

We will now show you how to find an honest, well-financed dealer—one you both like and trust—who is willing to give you the time and expert advice you need.

First, do not be overly impressed with the size of the dealer's company. The biggest companies are not necessarily the best. In fact, one of the largest coin dealers in the country is known by others to have been overcharging the public for years. Firms with from four to ten professional employees usually are much better. They need your business more, will work harder for you, and generally will give you better prices because they have lower overhead.

The initial contact may come from any source—the recommendation of associates, someone you hear about on a radio or TV show, the author of a good book—but in your initial inquiries, do not hesitate to ask as many questions as necessary to satisfy yourself about the individual and the firm. After all, it is your money that is at risk, and if the people you talk to are unable or unwilling to answer your concerns in an open manner (even to saying, "I don't know but I will sure find out"), that in itself should be a cause for suspicion. People who have nothing to hide most often will respect the legitimacy of your concerns and do their best to satisfy them.

## A 12-POINT CHECKLIST

Before you talk to anyone, prepare a written list of the questions you are going to ask. The following is a sampling of the kinds of questions to ask. Some of them will be answered before you express them but there are reasons why all of these things are important in one way or another:

1. How long have you been in business? Just being a relatively new company is not necessarily a negative. Keep in mind that longevity can also reveal a long record of lawsuits, indictments, misrepresentations, and the like. This question is good as an icebreaker but the next one is much more important.

2. What is the background and expertise of both the principals of the firm and the professional staff member(s) with whom I will be dealing? Try to determine whether these persons have had enough experience in numismatics positions, professional or otherwise (perhaps as long-time coin collectors or investors), so that they should know most of the U.S. coin types and varieties and the intricacies of the grading and pricing systems.

3. How are employees compensated? Are they solely commission salespeople or do they receive a salary plus a bonus based upon the sales they produce? Alternatively, do all of the dealer's employees receive fixed salaries, perhaps with profit sharing and stock bonuses based upon the success of the firm? Employees whose personal financial fortunes depend upon the success of their employer's company will tend to be far more aware of the customer's needs and will work harder to build long-term customer relationships than salespeople who are compensated on the basis of what they sell.

4. What are the specialties of the organization? These, of course, should include the areas that interest you, but beyond this, one will usually get the best service when the specialties of the firm do not go too

far beyond your own interests. A company that trades in both stamps and coins or coins and bullion, for example, or one that claims a worldwide expertise in ancient and modern coins will probably not serve you as well as a smaller firm whose specialties are closer to your own interests.

5. How are markups and markdowns determined? This is a difficult question, especially for a small company where markups and markdowns may be set on an informal sliding scale, with smaller percentages but larger dollar amounts on the more expensive items. However, an honest dealer will admit this and be willing to provide approximations for, say, a $5,000 and a $25,000 coin.

6. Do you have a written policy covering return of coins? Some firms will allow coins to be sent back, but only under certain conditions. One large dealer we know will permit coins to be returned within a reasonable period of time but they will only allow credit against future purchases, no cash refunds. Others will not permit the return, for any reason, of coins that were examined before purchase. A dealer that has a written policy allowing coins to be returned within a reasonable period of time and for a wide range of possible reasons will generally be found to be a firm that one can deal with comfortably.

7. Do you maintain a coin inventory or do you usually buy to fill customers' orders? Recognize that the capital necessary to maintain a large coin inventory costs a great deal of money, and one way or another that cost must be passed on to the customer or the dealer will go broke. It is usually best to trade with a dealer who buys primarily to fill orders but who occasionally will purchase a coin (or an entire collection) if it is offered at a bargain price, confident that current customers will purchase the coins when they learn what is available. Also, a dealer who maintains an inventory may be inclined at one time or another to "push" certain coins strictly to clear his inventory and not because it is in the best interests of his clients.

8. If the company says that it maintains an inventory, ask for specifics about how the inventory is financed. Do they use bank financing? Are their needs met with open lines of credit, or does the bank require that their financed inventory be stored in the bank's vaults?

9. Request bank references and the names of bank officers you might contact to confirm the nature of the dealer's relationships. You

may choose not to call these people but any reputable businessperson will not hesitate to provide such references to a prospective customer. If a dealer you are considering using refuses this request, consider it a negative to be further investigated. Ask yourself—and perhaps others—does that firm have something to hide?

10. Ask whether or not they would object to your contacting one or two of their customers as references. They will select customers they think will give them a good recommendation, of course, but this is something like asking for the names of former employers when interviewing a job applicant. One can learn a great deal by reading between the lines when a reference is contacted, and the very fact of being willing (or unwilling) to provide references may be an indication of whether the dealer thinks their customers generally are pleased with the service they have received. The nature of the response you receive when asking about customer references is more important than whether or not you are given names to call. The anonymity that reputable dealers provide their clients is very important, and you should consider it a favorable response if the person you are talking to is unwilling to breach this. Probably the best answer you can receive is to be told that, as a matter of company policy, they cannot provide you with customer references without first calling the customers themselves to be sure that there are no objections.

11. Along with bank references and customer references, ask for the names of legal firm(s) and individual attorneys that are used most often, and the length of time these firms have represented the dealer.

12. Finally, by all means ask what organizations the company belongs to. Four that responsible dealers are associated with are:

The INDUSTRY COUNCIL FOR TANGIBLE ASSETS (ICTA), 25 "E" Street NW, Washington, DC 20001; telephone 202-783-3500. This is the principal organization that serves to self-regulate the rare coin and bullion industries.

The BETTER BUSINESS BUREAU. In every community, the BBB is the organization that keeps a record of complaints about the business practices in their area. One or two complaints does not necessarily mean that you should not do business with a company. After all, there are usually two sides to any dispute. However, if a firm has had numerous complaints from former customers, for whatever reason(s), it probably is wise not to use them.

The CHAMBER OF COMMERCE. Always a good way to find out whether the company really exists and what its reputation is in the city where it is located.

The AMERICAN NUMISMATIC ASSOCIATION (ANA), 818 N. Cascade Avenue, Colorado Springs, Colorado 80903; telephone 719-632-2646. This organization is the oldest and largest of the many that concern themselves with coin collecting and coin investing. The principals of the firm you use should be members.

This may seem like a lot of questions to ask in the process of selecting a coin dealer. They probably could all be boiled down to asking: Who are you? And why should I buy from you? However, deciding who you will use to buy and sell coins for you is *the* most important decision you will ever make about investing in rare coins. It should not be entered into lightly.

Having said all of this, though, we recognize that ultimately the choice will hinge on a final question that each investor must ask, not of the dealer, but of himself: Is this a person and a firm I believe I could deal with over a period of years, comfortably and with confidence? If you have selected the right person and firm, you will find that your comfort and confidence grow with each contact and with each trade. If they don't, do not hesitate to start over again and select a different dealer.

# Chapter **4**

# COIN GRADING— CHANGES THAT HAVE GIVEN THE MARKET CONSISTENCY

You can now buy coins through your dealer "sight unseen." What this means is that when your dealer places an order for coins offered on the American Numismatic Exchange (ANE) or on the Certified Coin Exchange (CCE), you can have complete confidence that you will receive the exact coins and grades of coins that you have instructed the dealer to buy, even though neither you nor the dealer have physically examined those coins.

This method of trading was not possible prior to 1986, when the Professional Coin Grading Service (PCGS) began its independent and reliable service to the coin industry. Prior to that date, each and every coin had to be carefully examined by a prospective purchaser or his dealer representative before any transaction could take place. This was necessary, in part, in order to authenticate the coin, to be sure it was not counterfeit. But, in addition, the condition grade assigned by the seller had to be questioned closely to be sure that the purchaser agreed.

Today, authentication and grade are guaranteed so long as one buys only coins certified by PCGS or the Numismatic Guaranty Corporation of America (NGC).

The subjective manner in which grading was done in the past kept many people away from coins as an investment. All too often, those who did enter this market realized when it came time to sell that they had paid too much when they originally bought their coins, believing them to be of higher quality than prospective new purchasers would accept.

Walter H. Breen, a widely quoted numismatic scholar, observes that, "The novice who spends tens of thousands of dollars on coins is getting a very expensive education. What many of them learn that way is that they've been swindled."

Before dependable grading became a reality, coins were good investments for truly knowledgeable experts but they were not suitable as public investments, simply because the layman had no way of knowing for sure the quality of what he was buying—and the market prices of coins vary greatly with quality.

## TOWARD A STANDARDIZED TERMINOLOGY

The history of coin grading is a fascinating story in itself. Undoubtedly, the earliest coin transactions hinged on very broad condition terms, more a matter of individuals' subjective assessments than anything that could be put into words. It is easy to envision someone trying to sell a "perfect" example of a particular coin, only to have a prospective buyer look at it as "pretty good." When price came into play, of course, there would have been the haggling that goes into any commercial transaction. Little by little, though, out of necessity, condition terminology became more and more precise.

Numismatic coins always fall into one of two basic conditions. Either they are *circulated*—coins exhibiting wear from having changed hands many times in commercial transactions—or they are *uncirculated*. A numismatist always will make the distinction between circulated and uncirculated coins. For the most part, investors concentrate on uncirculated coins, while collectors often acquire both.

Over the years, several methods of coin grading have been adopted by numismatists. Today the most universally accepted terminology scale is the one endorsed by the American Numismatic Association.

ANA divides circulated and uncirculated coins into 24 distinct grades. There are 13 circulated grades and 11 uncirculated grades. The lowest circulated grade is *Poor-1;* the highest is *Choice About Uncirculated-58.* The uncirculated grades range from *MS-60* at the bottom of the scale to *MS-70* at the top, with the "MS" standing for *Mint State.* Figures 4 and 5, on pages 40 and 41, give the complete listings of the ANA grading standards, together with verbal descriptions of the coin condition implied by each grading term.

The word "proof" denotes a coin that began with a highly polished coin blank, or planchet, that is struck, more slowly and with higher pressure, with specially prepared dies at least twice to ensure that the strike is full and sharp. Most proof coins minted today are called "cameo proofs." These are manufactured by special techniques and are for the purpose of sale to numismatic collectors. To prepare a cameo proof coin, the area of the die that creates the background (this is called the "field") is highly polished, while the area of the die that is used to create the raised image or "device" remains rough and unpolished since it is recessed. The devices will eventually become more polished from subsequent striking. Thus a cameo is a proof of an early strike. The result is a coin with a mirrorlike field and a frosty-appearing device.

While, technically, a proof coin might have been circulated, most of them are acquired by collectors and investors and are never used for commercial purchases. The word means a method of manufacture rather than the condition of a coin. Proof coins are given the same numeric condition grades as other high quality uncirculated coins, preceded by "PR" in place of "MS."

We must always remember that grading is used only as a shorthand way of describing the condition of a specific uncirculated (or proof) coin. This means *all* of the following:

- A coin of a certain type and denomination (for example, a Morgan Dollar),
- Bearing a specific mintage date (perhaps 1888),
- Possibly imprinted with a mint mark to show where it was struck
    P or no mint mark—Philadelphia (the "Mother Mint")
    S—San Francisco
    CC—Carson City (Nevada)
    D—Denver

O—New Orleans
W—West Point (New York)
C—Charlotte (North Carolina)
D—Dahlonega (Georgia)

- Further subdivisions that are customarily applied only to specific coin types (For example, with Mercury Dimes only, the further designation "FSB" means with "Fully Split Bands"), and, finally,

- The numeric grade, from "60" to "70," that has been determined to best characterize the condition of that coin.

R.S. Yeoman's "Red Book" (*A Guide Book of United States Coins*) includes a generalized guide to specific locations on different coin types where points of wear, etc., will be found in order to justify a particular grade assignment. These guidelines are available for your information but the advent of a standardized grading process has eliminated the need for the investor to become an expert in grading.

## COMPUTER GRADING WILL MAKE A GREAT CONCEPT EVEN BETTER

Ultimately, grading is a subjective evaluation of condition. The grade assigned in a particular examination is open to question unless the person doing the grading: 1) has had a long period of training in looking at coins under the tutelage of members of the small fraternity of real experts; and 2) is honest and disinterested in the results of his examination. When these two conditions are not met, variability in the application of standards cannot be avoided.

Even before they began using computers for grading purposes, PCGS and NGC had established themselves as being reliable, honest, and consistent in their assignment of condition grades. This was a great improvement over the prior situation, where a prospective purchaser often had to face a dealer who, perhaps, did not know the intricacies of grading, and thus made frequent mistakes. Under such circumstances, the buyer could not help but question whether the dealer had a built-in bias in favor of grading the coins he was selling as high as possible. In fact, PCGS has recently undergone three years of scrutiny by the Federal Trade Commission (FTC). The result of this investigation was that PCGS signed a consent agreement that essentially stated that they should continue to do business in the manner that they have been since

## UNCIRCULATED GRADES OF U.S. COINS

| Grade | Contact Marks | Hairlines | Luster | Eye Appeal |
|---|---|---|---|---|
| MS-70 | none show under magnification | None show under magnification | Very attractive Fully original | Outstanding |
| MS-69 | 1 or 2 miniscule none in prime focal areas | None visible | Very attractive Fully original | Exceptional |
| MS-68 | 3 or 4 miniscule none in prime focal areas | None visible | Attractive Fully original | Exceptional |
| MS-67 | 3 or 4 miniscule 1 or 2 may be in prime focal areas | None visible without magnification | Above average Fully original | Exceptional |
| MS-66 | Several small; a few may be in prime focal areas | None visible without magnification | Above average Fully original | Above average |
| MS-65 | Light and scattered without major distracting marks in prime focal areas | May have a few scattered | Fully original | Very pleasing |
| MS-64 | May have light scattered marks; a few may be in prime focal areas | May have a few scattered or small patch in secondary areas | Average Fully original | Pleasing |
| MS-63 | May have distracting marks in prime focal areas | May have a few scattered or small patch | May be original or slightly impaired | Rather attractive |
| MS-62 | May have distracting marks in prime and/or secondary areas | May have a few scattered to noticeable patch | May be original or impaired | Occasionally acceptable |
| MS-61 | May have a few heavy (or numerous light) marks in prime focal and/or secondary areas | May have noticeable patch or continuous hairlining over surfaces | May be original or impaired | Unattractive |
| MS-60 | May have heavy marks in all areas | May have noticeable patch or continuous hairlining throughout | May be original or impaired | Poor |

Source: *Official A.N.A. Grading Standards for the United States Coins*, 3rd edition, American Numismatic Association, 1988

Figure 4

# CIRCULATED GRADES OF U.S. COINS

| Grade | Description of Grade | Description including contact marks, hairlines, luster and eye appeal |
|---|---|---|
| AU-58 | Very Choice About Uncirculated-58 | The barest trace of wear may be seen on one or more of the high points of the design. No major detracting contact marks will be present and the coin will have attractive eye appeal and nearly full luster, with the appearance of a higher grade. |
| AU-55 | Choice About Uncirculated-55 | Only a small trace of wear is visible on the highest points of the coin. As in the case with the other grades here, wear often occurs in different spots on different designs. |
| AU-50 | About Uncirculated-50 | With traces of wear on nearly all of the highest areas. At least half of the original mint luster is present. |
| EF-45 | Choice Extremely Fine-45 | With light overall wear on the coin's highest points. All design details are very sharp. Mint luster is usually seen in the letter in protected areas of the coin's surface, such as between the star points and in the letter spaces. |
| EF-40 | Extremely Fine-40 | With only slight wear but more extensive than the preceding, still with excellent overall sharpness. Traces of mint luster may still show. |
| VF-30 | Choice Very Fine-30 | With light even wear on the surface, design details on the highest points lightly worn, but with all lettering and major features sharp. |
| VF-20 | Very Fine-20 | As preceding but with moderate wear on highest parts. |
| F-12 | Fine-12 | Moderate to considerable even wear. Entire design is bold. All lettering, including the word LIBERTY, if on a shield or headband, is only partially visible. |
| VG-8 | Very Good-8 | Well worn. Most fine details such as hair strands, leaf details and so on are worn nearly smooth. The word LIBERTY, if on a shield or headband is only partially visible. |
| G-4 | Good-4 | Heavily worn. Major designs visible, but with faintness areas. Head of Liberty, wreath, and other major features visible in outline form without center detail. |
| AG-3 | About Good-3 | Very heavily worn with portions of the lettering, date, and legends being worn smooth. The date barely readable. |
| P-1 | Poor | Nearly worn smooth. Identifiable only as to basic type. |

Source: *Official A.N.A. Grading Standards for the United States Coins,* 3rd edition, American Numismatic Association, 1988

Figure 5

their inception.

The first attempt at coin certification began in 1972, when the American Numismatic Association established ANACS, the American Numismatic Association Certification Service. Initially this was an authentication service, designed to advise collectors on whether their coins were genuine and whether or not they had been modified to make them appear to be in better condition than they really were. It was not until 1978 that ANACS began the additional service of grading coins that were submitted to them.

ANACS provides a reliable service—as far as it goes. It is a part of the ANA, the largest organization of its kind; it allows individuals to send coins in for authentication if they choose to, bypassing any dealer involvement; and, beyond a doubt, ANACS has the finest state-of-the-art equipment for authenticating coins. When coins are returned, they are accompanied by a photograph of the coin and a certificate of authenticity. ANACS has only recently started to encapsulate coins.

Coins authenticated or graded by ANACS are not traded on either the American Numismatic Exchange or the Certified Coin Exchange, and dealers do not buy ANACS-graded coins without seeing them first.

Many other coin grading services have appeared since ANACS. Most of them are not sufficiently well accepted to be worth mentioning. However, one that is fairly well known is the Numismatic Certification Institute, or NCI, located in Dallas, Texas, and operated by James Halperin. It is common knowledge among coin dealers that NCI still grades coins by old, outdated standards although they are still technically correct grades. Therefore, the grades of NCI coins can be quite liberal. This service is used extensively by telemarketing companies so that salespeople truthfully can tell a potential customer that what they are offering are "graded coins," with the implication that they are graded based on today's standards. The firm then can charge a much higher markup on their purchase prices than would be the case if the coins were assigned the grades other services would have given them. The customer who buys from such dealers will not know until it comes time to sell that no one else will buy their coins "sight unseen" and seldom will anyone grade them as high as when they were purchased.

The first major change leading toward rare coins possibly becoming a viable investment medium occurred in 1986, when David Hall established the Professional Coin Grading Service (PCGS) in Newport Beach, California. As of June 1, 1990, PCGS had certified 2,086,000 coins, submitted to them through a network of 552 dealers.

PCGS has more than 15 graders on their staff. A minimum of three must agree on the grade of any coin before the final grade is assigned. After a grade is determined, the coin is sonically sealed in an inert, hard plastic container, along with its description, grade, and unique serial number, and a hologram (similar to the ones found on major credit cards) and returned, through the dealer, to the customer. The service costs $26 per coin, plus postage and insurance, with several levels of express service available at extra cost. PCGS is not involved in the rare coin market. This is an authentication and grading service only, and it comes with a cash-backed guarantee.

PCGS recently announced that they have a new grading "expert" on their staff—a Macintosh® IIx running a 50 megahertz Motorola 68030 chip. Give their software/hardware package a Morgan Dollar, and three minutes and 2.2 billion calculations later you have a graded coin.

Knowing the advances in computer technology over the last five years, few numismatists seriously doubted that it ultimately could be done, but it took PCGS several years and several million dollars to accomplish the reality, a reality that started grading coins on May 17, 1990.

Forty-two coins can be examined during one cycle before the operator must turn the coins over for examination of the reverses. The computer holds the information on each obverse, matches it to the reverse data, and then determines the final grade at a rate of three minutes per coin, 24 hours a day (if desired), without error, eyestrain, or coffee breaks.

The software, of course, is the heart of the system. It uncannily replicates the decision-making process of a grader examining a coin, and it captures the subjective observation parameters of the human grader. In this sense, the machine is not objective—nor could it be because there is no mathematical description for an 1885-S Morgan dollar graded MS-65. However, this computer system does provide *subjective* grading that is *consistently applied* to all coins. Having been taught what the grades mean, it unerringly uses the knowledge within its programmed storage to grade coins dependably.

Can the human element be eliminated completely? Probably not—ever. However, the PCGS computer programs do grade coins far more rapidly and more dependably than humans. Investors can now buy any PCGS-graded coin with the same confidence they have had in the past concerning coins graded manually by PCGS.

Competition is, of course, the American way, and it was not long before the Numismatic Guaranty Corporation of America, or NGC, was established to perform services that are very similar to PCGS's. NGC is located in Parsippany, New Jersey, and also requires that coins be submitted through a network of more than 450 authorized dealers.

NGC has more than 15 graders on its staff and every coin is viewed by a grading team of three to five members. A finalizer assembles the grades and verifies the assigned grade. The finalizer must not be in the business of buying and selling coins.

The service costs a minimum of $23, plus postage and insurance. After a coin is graded, but before it is returned to the customer, it is sonically sealed in a "lab-tested," inert, hard plastic holder, along with its description, grade, and unique serial number and a hologram.

NGC will not grade coins dated after 1964. Their grading philosophy is designed to be strict no matter what condition the coin market is in. The principals do not buy or sell coins for commercial profit, and maintain a strict "arm's length" objectivity.

PCGS and NGC are similar in many respects. Both maintain grading sets for comparative purposes. PCGS, for example, has a grading set consisting of 500 coins that are referred to when grading coins to assure consistency in the grades assigned. In addition, both publish population reports that now are accepted by dealers and investors as the standards of rarity—a major factor in determining rare coin prices. NGC, so far, has not begun to use computers for grading but they undoubtedly will follow the lead of PCGS in this respect sometime in the not-too-distant future.

All PCGS and NGC dealers are independent contractors who are responsible for making their own markets in graded coins. Some of these are wholesalers, others maintain extensive retail inventories. By far the most significant impact on the market, though, has been by the dealer firms that are members of the American Numismatic Exchange (ANE) and the Certified Coin Exchange (CCE). The ANE and CCE marketmakers offer access to the national daily bid/ask market for PCGS and NGC-graded coins *sight unseen*.

Grading by PCGS and NGC has not reduced coin investing to the absolute interchangeability of product that is desirable for an investment commodity. The most rare, and thus the most expensive, coins still are seldom traded without the purchaser first examining them. However, the stability and dependability of PCGS and NGC grading has provided a floor for any particular coin date and grade, and this floor is now accepted by all reputable rare coin dealers as a reliable basis for sight-unseen trading.

The most important fact for an investor to remember, though, is that *only PCGS and NGC-graded coins* are traded sight unseen on the American Numismatic Exchange and on the Certified Coin Exchange. In other words, rare coins graded by one or the other of these two companies, *and no others*, are considered to be consistently and accurately graded. The investor should buy nothing else without first acquiring the expertise to personally grade coins—and that is a time-consuming and difficult task.

# Chapter 5

# UNDERSTANDING RARITY

It is critical to understand rarity as it relates to numismatics. Demand, prices, and the direction of the market are a direct result of rarity.

Rarity is a concept taken all too lightly by the average investor. It implies far more than just the age of a coin. Because a coin is 50–100 years old does not necessarily mean that it is rare, and even further from the truth is the assumption that it is worth a lot of money.

As with age, the number of coins originally produced may have little to do with their rarity. There are numerous factors that make a coin more rare or more common than would be suspected from the mintage figures alone. Mint records generally (though not always) give an indication of the maximum number of specimens of each particular type and year. But, keeping in mind our primary goal of profit performance, we must use the mint figures along with a knowledge of other political, economic, and social events that could be significant in determining the appreciation value of a coin.

A basic principle to keep in mind is that a rare coin is one that is difficult to find and, possibly, not even obtainable. This does not mean that it does not exist anymore (though with some coins this is a distinct possibility), but rather that it is extremely hard, if not impossible, to locate for purchase on the open market.

# CERTIFIED COIN POPULATION REPORTS

The population reports that are published each month by PCGS and bimonthly by NGC are carefully subdivided to show the numbers of coins that, to the date of the report, have been graded MS-60 to MS-70 and PR-60 to PR-70. Certain issues of the PCGS Population Report now include the populations of circulated coins and some foreign coins they now certify. As an example, we can look at Figure 6, which is a reproduction of one page from the April 1, 1990, PCGS Population Report—a page from the section of the book dealing with Morgan Dollars. If we look down the first column to PCGS No. 97199, we can make the following statement about the 1890-CC, MSPL Morgan Dollars (MSPL is a subdivision applicable only to Morgan Dollars that means "Mint State Proof-Like"—having a partial mirror-like surface or field): 95 of these coins have so far been graded by PCGS; and one of them has been graded MS-65, with none finer.

In other words, these PCGS population statistics, along with those in the NGC report, provide us with the total number of coins graded MS-60, MS-61, ... etc., to MS-70, by coin type and denomination, by date minted, by mint designation, and by any further subdivisions (such as the segregation of "Proof-like") that may be required.

The figures on the population reports are only approximations, of course, for many high-grade coins, so far, have not been submitted to either PCGS or NGC for grading, and the numbers may grow with each new report. Nevertheless, enough coins have now been graded that they do give us a reasonably good picture of the population curves for each coin type, date, and variety. And, most important, these are the *only* approximations we have of the total numbers of existing uncirculated mint state and proof coins.

When investigating the rarity of a particular coin, the number originally minted, as recorded in the annals of the United States Mint, is the starting point, and this number is given for each coin type in the *Red Book*. However, as we might expect, the numbers of uncirculated coins that still exist are almost always just a small fraction of the original number minted. For example, if we compare an Indian Head $10 Gold Eagle that does not have on the reverse the motto, "In God We Trust," with the later (after 1908) version that does have the motto, we

# Wealth Building in the 90s

## PCGS POPULATION REPORT SAMPLE PAGE

Page No.   73                 PCGS Population Report, Copyright 1990                    04/01/90

| PCGS No | Date | Denom | Variety | DSIG | 60 | 61 | 62 | 63 | 64 | 65 | 66 | 67 | 68 | 69 | 70 |
|---|---|---|---|---|---|---|---|---|---|---|---|---|---|---|---|
| 97181 | 1887-S | S$1 | | MSDM | 1 | 4 | 5 | 12 | 2 | 0 | 0 | 0 | 0 | 0 | 0 |
| 7182 | 1888 | S$1 | | MS | 32 | 93 | 558 | 2765 | 2663 | 709 | 21 | 1 | 0 | 0 | 0 |
| 7183 | 1888 | S$1 | | MSPL | 2 | 7 | 25 | 51 | 27 | 10 | 3 | 0 | 0 | 0 | 0 |
| 97183 | 1888 | S$1 | | MSDM | 2 | 4 | 19 | 31 | 33 | 11 | 1 | 0 | 0 | 0 | 0 |
| 7184 | 1888-O | S$1 | | MS | 45 | 110 | 574 | 1788 | 1161 | 240 | 4 | 0 | 0 | 0 | 0 |
| 7185 | 1888-O | S$1 | | MSPL | 7 | 21 | 42 | 96 | 64 | 13 | 0 | 0 | 0 | 0 | 0 |
| 97185 | 1888-O | S$1 | | MSDM | 4 | 9 | 30 | 73 | 49 | 13 | 0 | 0 | 0 | 0 | 0 |
| 7186 | 1888-S | S$1 | | MS | 47 | 114 | 272 | 405 | 206 | 37 | 1 | 0 | 0 | 0 | 0 |
| 7187 | 1888-S | S$1 | | MSPL | 1 | 5 | 19 | 39 | 11 | 0 | 0 | 0 | 0 | 0 | 0 |
| 97187 | 1888-S | S$1 | | MSDM | 2 | 5 | 17 | 33 | 14 | 1 | 0 | 0 | 0 | 0 | 0 |
| 7188 | 1889 | S$1 | | MS | 52 | 143 | 827 | 2461 | 1498 | 220 | 5 | 3 | 0 | 0 | 0 |
| 7189 | 1889 | S$1 | | MSPL | 0 | 5 | 26 | 42 | 21 | 2 | 0 | 0 | 0 | 0 | 0 |
| 97189 | 1889 | S$1 | | MSDM | 1 | 6 | 10 | 28 | 9 | 1 | 0 | 0 | 0 | 0 | 0 |
| 7190 | 1889-CC | S$1 | | MS | 10 | 17 | 39 | 19 | 6 | 1 | 0 | 0 | 0 | 0 | 0 |
| 7191 | 1889-CC | S$1 | | MSPL | 4 | 2 | 7 | 5 | 1 | 0 | 0 | 0 | 0 | 0 | 0 |
| 97191 | 1889-CC | S$1 | | MSDM | 4 | 8 | 9 | 8 | 1 | 0 | 0 | 0 | 0 | 0 | 0 |
| 7192 | 1889-O | S$1 | | MS | 31 | 85 | 270 | 419 | 215 | 23 | 2 | 0 | 0 | 0 | 0 |
| 7193 | 1889-O | S$1 | | MSPL | 0 | 3 | 12 | 20 | 7 | 3 | 0 | 0 | 0 | 0 | 0 |
| 97193 | 1889-O | S$1 | | MSDM | 2 | 1 | 9 | 12 | 5 | 1 | 0 | 0 | 0 | 0 | 0 |
| 7194 | 1889-S | S$1 | | MS | 30 | 106 | 301 | 594 | 379 | 94 | 6 | 0 | 0 | 0 | 0 |
| 7195 | 1889-S | S$1 | | MSPL | 4 | 3 | 21 | 34 | 13 | 2 | 0 | 0 | 0 | 0 | 0 |
| 97195 | 1889-S | S$1 | | MSDM | 1 | 4 | 6 | 7 | 4 | 0 | 0 | 0 | 0 | 0 | 0 |
| 7196 | 1890 | S$1 | | MS | 43 | 139 | 574 | 1207 | 406 | 20 | 0 | 0 | 0 | 0 | 0 |
| 7197 | 1890 | S$1 | | MSPL | 2 | 7 | 23 | 24 | 10 | 1 | 0 | 0 | 0 | 0 | 0 |
| 97197 | 1890 | S$1 | | MSDM | 1 | 7 | 25 | 23 | 9 | 1 | 0 | 0 | 0 | 0 | 0 |
| 7198 | 1890-CC | S$1 | | MS | 68 | 168 | 356 | 458 | 177 | 30 | 2 | 0 | 0 | 0 | 0 |
| 7199 | 1890-CC | S$1 | | MSPL | 5 | 16 | 40 | 27 | 6 | 1 | 0 | 0 | 0 | 0 | 0 |
| 97199 | 1890-CC | S$1 | | MSDM | 18 | 22 | 64 | 59 | 23 | 4 | 0 | 0 | 0 | 0 | 0 |
| 7200 | 1890-O | S$1 | | MS | 35 | 135 | 487 | 1129 | 596 | 61 | 2 | 0 | 0 | 0 | 0 |
| 7201 | 1890-O | S$1 | | MSPL | 5 | 16 | 48 | 85 | 31 | 5 | 0 | 0 | 0 | 0 | 0 |
| 97201 | 1890-O | S$1 | | MSDM | 2 | 4 | 24 | 51 | 33 | 3 | 0 | 0 | 0 | 0 | 0 |
| 7202 | 1890-S | S$1 | | MS | 59 | 131 | 455 | 808 | 513 | 140 | 26 | 0 | 0 | 0 | 0 |
| 7203 | 1890-S | S$1 | | MSPL | 4 | 7 | 25 | 38 | 8 | 3 | 0 | 0 | 0 | 0 | 0 |
| 97203 | 1890-S | S$1 | | MSDM | 2 | 6 | 11 | 15 | 6 | 3 | 0 | 0 | 0 | 0 | 0 |
| 7204 | 1891 | S$1 | | MS | 45 | 118 | 391 | 453 | 169 | 14 | 1 | 0 | 0 | 0 | 0 |
| 7205 | 1891 | S$1 | | MSPL | 2 | 3 | 12 | 7 | 3 | 0 | 0 | 0 | 0 | 0 | 0 |
| 97205 | 1891 | S$1 | | MSDM | 0 | 1 | 3 | 8 | 2 | 0 | 0 | 0 | 0 | 0 | 0 |
| 7206 | 1891-CC | S$1 | | MS | 134 | 250 | 631 | 927 | 400 | 62 | 4 | 0 | 0 | 0 | 0 |
| 7207 | 1891-CC | S$1 | | MSPL | 3 | 34 | 56 | 51 | 33 | 5 | 0 | 0 | 0 | 0 | 0 |
| 97207 | 1891-CC | S$1 | | MSDM | 12 | 16 | 28 | 33 | 4 | 1 | 0 | 0 | 0 | 0 | 0 |
| 7208 | 1891-O | S$1 | | MS | 30 | 90 | 260 | 443 | 154 | 12 | 0 | 0 | 0 | 0 | 0 |
| 7209 | 1891-O | S$1 | | MSPL | 1 | 1 | 5 | 10 | 0 | 0 | 0 | 0 | 0 | 0 | 0 |
| 97209 | 1891-O | S$1 | | MSDM | 0 | 1 | 5 | 1 | 0 | 1 | 0 | 0 | 0 | 0 | 0 |
| 7210 | 1891-S | S$1 | | MS | 36 | 68 | 308 | 525 | 341 | 84 | 6 | 4 | 0 | 0 | 0 |
| 7211 | 1891-S | S$1 | | MSPL | 2 | 18 | 32 | 64 | 29 | 3 | 0 | 0 | 0 | 0 | 0 |
| 97211 | 1891-S | S$1 | | MSDM | 2 | 4 | 12 | 16 | 9 | 0 | 0 | 0 | 0 | 0 | 0 |
| 7212 | 1892 | S$1 | | MS | 18 | 43 | 172 | 331 | 180 | 40 | 0 | 0 | 0 | 0 | 0 |
| 7213 | 1892 | S$1 | | MSPL | 0 | 2 | 2 | 11 | 6 | 2 | 0 | 0 | 0 | 0 | 0 |
| 97213 | 1892 | S$1 | | MSDM | 1 | 3 | 7 | 7 | 4 | 1 | 0 | 0 | 0 | 0 | 0 |
| 7214 | 1892-CC | S$1 | | MS | 60 | 114 | 317 | 360 | 172 | 41 | 5 | 1 | 0 | 0 | 0 |
| 7215 | 1892-CC | S$1 | | MSPL | 14 | 17 | 47 | 34 | 9 | 5 | 0 | 0 | 0 | 0 | 0 |
| 97215 | 1892-CC | ·S$1 | | MSDM | 7 | 12 | 21 | 17 | 2 | 0 | 0 | 0 | 0 | 0 | 0 |
| 7216 | 1892-O | S$1 | | MS | 29 | 73 | 333 | 718 | 285 | 21 | 0 | 0 | 0 | 0 | 0 |
| 7217 | 1892-O | S$1 | | MSPL | 0 | 0 | 1 | 2 | 2 | 0 | 0 | 0 | 0 | 0 | 0 |

Figure 6

have the following population numbers:

|  | Original Mintage | Population Estimate MS-63 to MS-68* |
|---|---|---|
| No Motto $10 Indian | 483,400 | 346 |
| With Motto $10 Indian | 14,285,000 | 4,383 |

(*PCGS Population Report, April 1, 1990)

In order to maximize your earnings, you want to acquire the rarest coins that you can afford. To determine which coin types and dates are most rare, and thus worth the most money, you cannot just look at the original mintage figures, for the number that have survived, as a percentage of the coins originally minted, vary greatly from one coin type to another and from one date to another for the same coin type.

To further illustrate this variability in survival rates, we prepared Figure 7, comparing the numbers of 1888 to 1891 Morgan Dollars originally minted with the numbers graded MS-60 or above by PCGS. Out of the 700,000 minted at the San Francisco Mint in 1889, at least 1,609 exist today in mint state, but only 1,563 remain out of 5,296,000 produced at that Mint in 1891.

A majority of the coins that are now being sought for investment purposes were minted in large quantities and intended for circulation, but for some reason or another were never released for that purpose. In these situations we need to have an understanding of the whole picture.

For example, there were only 20 proofs minted of the 1878 $3 Gold Piece, but there were 82,000 "business strikes," intended to be used as currency. The original mintage of 82,000, though a relatively small number as compared to many other coins, was the second largest number produced in any year of that coin's existence, from 1854 to 1889. But this is not a clear indication of the coin's rarity. Other factors have reduced that number to only 1,300 investment-quality survivors, graded MS-60 to MS-67. The better the condition, the lower the survival rate.

It is the number of coins that have survived that is most important. For this reason, the PCGS and NGC Population Reports are invaluable as tools in understanding rarity. However, the figures from these reports may not necessarily indicate the whole story. For instance, you should

## VARIABILITY OF SURVIVAL RATE
### 1888–1891 Morgan Dollars

| Year/ Mint | Quantity Minted[1] | Quantity Certified[2] |
|---|---|---|
| 1888 | 19,183,832 | 7,168 |
| 1888-O | 12,150,000 | 4,343 |
| 1888-S | 657,000 | 1,229 |
| | | |
| 1889 | 21,726,811 | 5,360 |
| 1889-CC | 350,000 | 141 |
| 1889-O | 11,875,000 | 1,120 |
| 1889-S | 700,000 | 1,609 |
| | | |
| 1890 | 16,802,590 | 2,522 |
| 1890-CC | 2,309,041 | 1,543 |
| 1890-O | 10,701,000 | 2,752 |
| 1890-S | 8,230,373 | 2,260 |
| | | |
| 1891 | 8,694,206 | 1,232 |
| 1891-CC | 1,618,000 | 2,684 |
| 1891-O | 7,954,529 | 1,014 |
| 1891-S | 5,296,000 | 1,563 |

[1]From R.S. Yeoman: *A Guide Book of United States Coins*, 43rd Edition, 1990
[2]From *PCGS Population Report*, April 1, 1990 (Figure 6)

Figure 7

bear in mind that for a variety of reasons, including the quality of a mint's equipment, the planchets, die pressures, etc., all coins were *not* struck such that they would have been graded Mint State 65, 66, 67, or better. Many coins, when they rolled off the presses, would be hard pressed (no pun intended) to qualify as Mint State 63.

It is for reasons such as these that the wise investor should rely on an experienced dealer to plan and select the proper rare coins for a portfolio commensurate with your investment goals.

## FACTORS INFLUENCING RARITY

Numerous factors combine to determine what is truly a "rare" coin at any point in time.

Original Mintage

The numbers of a particular coin originally minted, of course, provide a maximum limit. The 1804 dollar is an interesting example of how even the numbers that *supposedly* were minted originally can be confusing.

There are two varieties of dollars bearing the date of "1804," and neither of these appear to have been actually minted in that year. Those that are called the "Originals" (of which eight are known to exist) were struck at the mint in the 1834–35 period, in order to complete proof sets that were given as presentation gifts to foreign dignitaries. Then, in 1859, the pieces known as "Restrikes" (of which seven are known) were minted to supply the needs of collectors who wanted specimens in order to complete their sets. Although mint records state that 19,570 dollars were coined in 1804, the probability is that those actually produced in 1804 bore the date of 1803. Needless to say, the extreme rarity of the 1804 U.S. dollar has led to the production of a large number of counterfeits.

In addition to the variation in numbers originally minted and unusual circumstances such as with the 1804 dollar, there are also several other kinds of social/economic/political events that have combined to severely restrict the numbers of most extant coins.

The 1933 Gold Confiscation Act

Probably the act that had the greatest impact of all, not only on the history of numismatics but on the economy as well, was the Gold Surrender Order of 1933. On March 6, 1933, President Franklin D. Roosevelt issued an order that prohibited private ownership of gold bullion by American citizens, with a few exceptions given for industrial and commercial uses.

Roosevelt had taken office in 1932. At that time the entire world was suffering the effects of the Great Depression. Businesses were failing, people were losing their homes and farms, and unemployment ran as high as 50%. Roosevelt launched many new programs in a fervent effort to end the Great Depression.

One was the devaluation of the dollar, in the hope that it would stimulate the economy. Until that time, the United States had been on a gold standard, defined as a national currency based upon a fixed weight of gold. To accomplish the devaluation of the dollar, the official price of gold was raised from $20.67 per ounce to a fixed value of $35 per ounce. However, before this action was taken, and in order to prevent speculators from making major profits in gold, the Gold Surrender Order/Confiscation Act was issued. This stated, in part, that "no person other than a Federal Reserve Bank ... shall acquire in the United States gold coin, gold bullion or gold certificates except under license therefore issued pursuant to this Executive Order." In addition, the order included strict restrictions on those who were allowed to use gold for trade or business.

Because most people did not understand the specific exceptions of this order, millions of U.S. gold coins were surrendered to the government at face value and subsequently melted down. This was also an era of patriotic values and many people felt it was their duty to obey this order and turn in their gold coins.

The Federal Reserve, the U.S. Treasury, and many banks were also the holders of large quantities of gold coins, which by law were surrendered and subsequently melted. Many coins dated from the 1920s to the early 1930s were destroyed, creating some priceless rarities today. One example is the 1931 Double Eagle: out of an original mintage of 2,938,250 there are only 100 survivors known today. The 1927 Double Eagle has a comparable mintage but is common. This is because this issue was not melted down as a result of the 1933 act.

Another rarity is the 1933 Double Eagle. A total of 445,500 were minted, according to U.S. Mint records, but none of these coins was ever released for circulation. A few, however, found their way out of the Mint's vaults and into the private sector. When it became known that these coins had slipped through the cracks, the Treasury Department declared it illegal for anyone to possess the coin, and the only known examples are encased in the Smithsonian Institution's National Numismatic Collection. Incidentally, this in the only U.S. gold coin that is still illegal for any private individual to own.

After World War I, the United States had sent millions of dollars in gold coins to help rebuild the European countries. When the U.S. began to melt down their remaining gold coins in the 1930s, the Europeans were smart enough to keep what they had in coin form. As a result, 90% of the gold coins we have today ultimately resurfaced in Europe and were sold to collectors and investors here in later years.

When gold coins were in circulation, they were minted in much smaller quantities than the lower denomination silver, nickel, and copper coins. Because of their higher face value, gold coins also were more expensive to save for collection purposes. Finally, gold is a significantly softer metal than silver, nickel, or copper, so gold coins become nicked, scratched, and marked much easier.

With all of the gold coins that were destroyed, melted down, or lost, only those that escaped to Europe and those hidden by private individuals in the United States remain. It wasn't until the end of 1974 that Congress passed legislation once again legalizing the ownership of gold by U.S. citizens.

Gold coins are the rarest of United States coins in top condition. Today, 85% of those that survive are below investment quality or MS-60. For all of these reasons, the MS-64 and MS-65 gold coins you buy today could well be the museum pieces of tomorrow.

Silver Dollars from 1878 to 1935

The United States silver dollars minted between 1878 and 1935 provide an entirely different picture of political/economic actions that have had a tremendous impact upon rarity. They are the world's most popular coins, and the subject of considerable controversy within the numismatic community.

The difference between silver dollars and all other U.S. coins is *availability*. Silver dollars are the most readily available U.S. rare coins.

The political history behind the minting of the unnecessarily large quantities of silver dollars has been documented in several silver dollar books. The basic principle is the most important factor to comprehend in order to understand the silver dollar market.

Silver dollars were never a popular coinage in the Eastern United States. They are large, bulky coins that were as cumbersome to carry in one's pockets 100 years ago as Ike dollars are today. However, out West cowboys loved them. They could carry silver dollars in their saddle bags and not have to be bothered with small coinage which was easily lost out of their pockets.

Why did the government mint so many coins that clearly were not needed for commercial reasons except in a few sparsely populated Western States like Wyoming, Nevada, Montana, etc.? It was simply a political favor to the Western mining and cattle interests and to their Eastern bankers. Under the authority of several different Congressional acts, the government agreed to purchase between two and five million ounces of silver per month. The silver that was purchased continued to be minted into silver dollars, and these uncirculated silver dollars sat around in treasury vaults gathering dust for more than half a century. Today issues such as the 1880-CC, 1881-CC and 1885-CC are far more common in MS-63 through MS-65 condition than their low mintage figures would indicate.

Because silver dollars were minted in mega-quantities, they are now the most available U.S. rare coin. Twenty years ago, you could acquire all the silver dollars you could want, at face value, from any bank or from the U.S. Treasury. Since then, the popularity of collecting this coin has gradually driven the prices somewhat higher but even rare date Morgan Dollars can still be found. It is only when one searches for the higher-grade specimens, in MS-65 or better condition, and better dates that they seem to be rare.

Other Social Factors

Strange as it may seem, some coins are now rare due to having been exported. From 1873 to 1885, certain issues of silver dollars produced in the United States were coined for the specific purpose of providing a trade currency in the Orient. These dollars, called "Trade Dollars," weighed 420 grains compared to 412-1/2 grains of previous issues. The original 1873 mintage Trade Dollars were not legal tender in the United States, and almost all were shipped to the Orient, where they were "chopmarked" by merchants to determine that they were actually silver. With numerous chop marks as they passed from hand to hand, most of these coins were eventually destroyed. Today, it is difficult if not impossible to obtain an 1876-CC Trade Dollar graded MS-60 or better.

One final example of social factors influencing rarity: During the Great Depression, which lasted from 1929 to about 1939 (or later in some countries), the average U.S. citizen could not afford to hoard or collect high-grade coins. Those minted during this period have thus become extremely rare in the higher grades and denominations. As in any period of economic turmoil, the coinage that was available was used. It turned over rapidly and today appears well worn.

## HOW TO USE THE POPULATION REPORTS

The PCGS Population Reports, as we have said, are published monthly, and the NGC Population Reports are published bimonthly. They are available for purchase, not just to dealers and other insiders but to anyone who wants to see them, either by subscription or by single issue.

The population reports provide lists of the continuously larger numbers of coins that have been sent in and graded uncirculated MS-60 to MS-70 by the two services. The population reports occasionally provide reports on circulated coins as well. Furthermore, MS-70 coins do not exist except for modern commemoratives that are not worthy of investment. Thus, they provide one of the two key information needs for the successful rare coin investor. The other is data on the pricing of specific issues, which we will cover in the next chapter.

If you understand the reliability of the population reports and how they provide us with the best indication we have of the true rarity of mint state and proof coins, when you have the opportunity to buy a particular coin you will know just how "rare" that coin is, and how to use this information to your direct financial benefit.

One of the things you should always look for when buying coins is low populations. In other words, if you are considering the purchase of a particular coin and you note from the PCGS Population Report that there have been only two or three of those coins graded, say, MS-67, and none graded MS-68 or above, it means that there are only two or three of those coins known to exist *at that grade*, and *none finer*. If you buy that coin you will have a true rarity.

This is somewhat like buying a Rembrandt or a Chagall or a Renoir. Although there are variations among the paintings produced by these artists, any of their paintings are rarities. You may pay too much for a Renoir, depending upon the condition of the market at the time of your purchase. But no matter what you pay, you know that you have something that is one of the finest in the world of art. You have bought the best or certainly one of the best and if you time your purchases and sales to take maximum advantage of the market, you will always make money.

With rare coins, buying low population/high quality will *always* make it possible for you to sell for top prices—and sometimes at premiums to the going market prices, just because someone is determined to have *that coin* at any price.

What is the low number that constitutes a rarity or a market? One of a kind, certainly. But what about three or four? How about a dozen? A mintage of three with two buyers is not a market. A mintage of 1,000 with 2,000 buyers is a *hot* market. But among gold coins, the $20 St. Gaudens Double Eagle is probably the most beautiful coin the U.S. has ever produced, and because of this, it is very popular. Even if not "rare" in absolute numbers, the St. Gaudens in mint state condition is always popular and saleable.

A recent PCGS Population Report shows that among the 1928 St. Gaudens that have been graded, 954 are MS-65. MS-65 is considered high quality for any gold coin, certainly investment quality, and it is unlikely that anyone will lose money on this coin, with the proper timing of the purchase and sale to take advantage of the market, even though 954 specimens have been certified by PCGS.

It is hard not to talk about the pricing of coins ahead of time, but in this case it is important. More of the 1928 St. Gaudens were originally minted than any other date. Approximately two years ago, this coin could have been purchased, in MS-65 condition, for about $1,200. Since then it has gone above $3,000 in price, and dropped to a bid price of about $2,400. But, even though there may be a total of, say, 8,000 of these coins in existence, rather than the 937 that PCGS has graded and sealed, if the market demand 10 years from now is such that 20,000 people are trying to buy it, then it is an incredible coin to buy now.

The point is that *any* St. Gaudens is a good coin to buy in MS-65 condition. A 1910 from the Denver Mint in MS-65 condition has a population of 37. It is more rare (and more expensive) than the 1928. A 1910 from the Philadelphia Mint is even more rare (and more expensive) with a population of nine. In fact, the 1910 from Philadelphia has just 41 that have been graded *MS-64* and the asking price is about $5,300 at the time of writing this. Is this a good bargain?

As you have no doubt realized by now, for any particular coin and date at least four factors combine to produce "value": condition or grade, the number of coins in that grade, the price asked for one of those coins, and the special demand that may exist for any particular coin at a given point in time.

It is the opinion of the authors that the investor in rare coins will *always* do the best by acquiring the *highest grade* and *lowest population* coins having the *greatest demand* that available resources allow. You will hear some dealers suggest that, for the same amount of money, you can acquire more coins by buying MS-63 or MS-64 grades rather than paying premium prices to acquire MS-65 or better. But you will find in almost every case that the dealers who recommend this strategy are the operators of neighborhood "Mom-and-Pop" coin stores that carry inventories of lower grade coins. These shops are in business primarily to serve the needs of collectors rather than investors. They maintain inventories of lower graded coins and they stay in business if they turn their inventories often. In other words, it is in the small dealer's interest to sell you lower grade coins.

It is true that you can acquire *more* coins, in absolute numbers, if you buy coins that are below what we have defined as "investment grade." You can acquire even more if you purchase circulated coins— say, Extra Fine or About Uncirculated. However, it has been demonstrated time and again that the coin *investor* who is truly interested in making the most money on his investment will do best if he buys high-quality coins. With silver, nickel, and copper coins, the minimum grade to look for should be MS-65 or better; with gold coins this is sometimes lowered to MS-64. This is clearly demonstrated by the comparison of price changes between 1985 and 1990 for a sampling of Type coins (Figure 8).

Every time you buy a rare coin, you should look for the highest graded/lowest population coins you can afford. We may not know, in absolute terms, the numbers of coins that exist in any grade. But, the population reports published by PCGS and NGC do give us a good approximation of those numbers at any point in time. And it is these low population coins that will make you the most money—always.

In real estate, there is a familiar saying that the investor needs to remember only three words—location, location, location. The same principle applies to investing in rare coins. Only the words are changed—quality, quality, quality. Always buy quality!

## COMPARISON OF PRICE INCREASES FOR UNCIRCULATED TYPE COINS

| TYPE COINS | MS-60 | | MS-63 | | MS-65 | |
|---|---|---|---|---|---|---|
| | 1985 | 1990 | 1985 | 1990 | 1985 | 1990 |
| 3¢ Silver Type II | $350 | $230 | $825 | $2,600 | $3,500 | $7,650 |
| 20¢ Piece | 640 | 575 | 1,800 | 1,800 | 5,400 | 10,250 |
| 50¢ No Motto | 435 | 425 | 975 | 1,500 | 4,650 | 11,000 |
| Trade Dollar | 500 | 500 | 1,400 | 1,400 | 4,950 | 16,500 |
| | 1,925 | 1,730 | 5,000 | 7,300 | 18,500 | 45,400 |

| TYPE COINS | PROOF-60 | | PROOF-65 | |
|---|---|---|---|---|
| | 1985 | 1990 | 1985 | 1990 |
| 3¢ Silver Type II | $775 | $575 | $5,000 | $10,750 |
| 20¢ Piece | 800 | 700 | 6,600 | 9,800 |
| 50¢ No Motto | 475 | 375 | 4,750 | 9,800 |
| Trade Dollar | 800 | 910 | 6,300 | 13,250 |
| | **2,850** | **2,560** | **22,650** | **43,600** |

Figure 8

# Chapter 6

# HOW COIN PRICES ARE DETERMINED

In prior chapters we have described what had to happen before there could be a dependable, rare coin investment market. Beginning in 1986, the first of the requirements began to be met with the reliable definition of the investment product as a result of PCGS grading. With the regular publication of the population reports, the second requirement was met: the continuous, public reporting of the quantity of product available. In this chapter, we talk about the third essential ingredient—pricing of the investment product.

In order for standardized grading to become a universally accepted procedure, it had to be acknowledged and supported by a network through which prices could be determined and made accessible to coin dealers. This has happened; such dealer networks are now operating. Reliable and current data on the prices at which coins are actually sold—by and for dealers—is now a reality. Again we cannot overemphasize the importance of working with a reliable dealer to keep you abreast of all market changes in pricing.

## HOW THE SYSTEM WORKS

The mechanisms through which coin prices are determined and made available to coin dealers are the American Numismatic Exchange (ANE) and the Certified Coin Exchange (CCE). These are two competing computerized networks that join hundreds of dealers across the country. Member dealers enter bid and ask data on mint state and proof grade coins into a satellite-linked computer, and can actually carry out buy and sell transactions with each other through each of the systems. The computer linkage is not important to this discussion and is being modified and upgraded almost continuously. However, the ANE and the CCE are now accepted by all major coin dealers as the standard sight-unseen pricing for most, though not all certified, rare coins.

We must keep in mind that this is a pricing structure evolving from days of old. A typical transaction in the past would involve an interested buyer and an interested seller, with the buyer stating how much he was willing to pay for a coin and the seller stating how much he would sell the coin for.

The theory still holds true today. The primary difference is that the market used to consist of an elite group of people who primarily collected coins for their beauty, for enjoyment, and for general appreciation. Financial gains were secondary and, anyway, they all had a pretty good idea of what a fair price should be.

The trading scenario would be at a coin show, auction, or other public meeting ground that would permit each interested party to make his own appraisal of the coins for sale. A truly impressive piece might require an interested buyer to raise his price. Conversely, a nicked or scratched coin with poor appeal might encourage a seller to drop his price. All of these negotiations were done with each party present, and final decisions were made that were satisfactory to all. This type of trading is still carried on but, in addition, provision now has been made for a new type of sight unseen, investor trading.

With the recent mass investor interest in rare coins and the ready availability of computer technology, the slow bartering form of exchange has been changed into a fast-paced, computer-networked marketplace. The transition has been bumpy at best, bombarded with the obstacles that must be endured during any period of rapid change.

The bartering process continues with the American Numismatic Exchange, but what was once done with a gentle touch of human hands and the appreciation of the eye of the ultimate buyer, is now done via a computerized network. This is critical for you as an investor, for now you can buy with complete confidence.

The Certified Coin Exchange (CCE) is a relatively new dealer-to-dealer computerized coin trading network that has been established to trade PCGS and NGC-certified coins sight unseen. For more than three years the American Numismatic Exchange (ANE) has been the only truly liquid U.S. rare coin marketplace. The new CCE system offers another sophisticated vehicle for dealer-to-dealer transactions. The competition between the two systems has already resulted in a lot of new software, and more will be created all the time as each exchange tries to get an edge.

The formation of CCE is a positive development for the coin investor. It provides another liquid market for certified U.S. coins. This makes the marketplace even more attractive to the Wall Street firms who have just started committing resources to certified rare coins, and reportedly have hundreds of millions of dollars on the sidelines earmarked for the rare coin market.

Both ANE and CCE maintain computer databases of dealer bids (offers to buy) and asks (offers to sell) on PCGS and NGC-certified coins. A member dealer must pay substantial monthly fees and either purchase or lease the proper computer equipment to participate. Some of the equipment involves a significant investment, including a dedicated satellite dish, which allows one to access the most current information available. About 200 of the largest dealers in the country belong to one or both of the exchanges, and many of them post bids or asks on a daily basis.

The way the system works can be illustrated by a theoretical transaction involving a Canadian Maple Leaf. This is a 24K gold bullion coin that has no numismatic value but will clearly demonstrate wholesale and retail pricing in the coin industry.

The wholesale buy and sell spread for a one-ounce Canadian Maple Leaf available to a dealer may be as follows:

<u>BID</u>            <u>ASK</u>
$400           $405

A buyer/investor wishes to purchase a Maple Leaf from a dealer. If the dealer had to pay the wholesale asking price to acquire the coin, he would have to price it to the buyer for, say, $410.

At the other end of a similar transaction, if an investor wished to sell a Maple Leaf to a dealer, the dealer would offer to buy it at a price of $395, so that he could, in turn, offer it on the wholesale market for the going bid price and realize some profit. The structure for the two transactions thus would be:

<u>BID</u>      Dealer      <u>ASK</u>
$400                   $405

<u>SALE PRICE</u>      Buyer Spread      <u>PURCHASE PRICE</u>
$395                                   $410

This is a normal business transaction and it does not in any way represent unscrupulous tactics. It is unrealistic to expect a dealer to trade at his cost. He could not remain in business without making a profit, and in order to make a profit, there must be markups and markdowns when coins are either sold or purchased from customers.

Stock markets throughout the world have gone through a history that is surprisingly similar to the coin market. Both determine prices on the basis of the bid prices that a prospective buyer is willing to pay and the ask prices that a willing seller demands, with the ultimate transaction price somewhere in between. There are some exceptions to this, with stocks as well as coins, but the fact remains that in any dependable investment market, prices are determined by the free interchange of the bid and ask of dealer specialists.

On the major stock exchanges, bid and ask prices are constantly changing, some by the minute, during each trading day. But, the most recent bid and ask prices on every security are available with every change appearing on the computer keyboards of all brokerage houses, even in the most remote branch offices. If the information is crucial to a potential client, brokers usually can obtain the bid and ask prices that each market maker currently has on the screen for any stock.

In addition to the availability of bid and ask prices, though, on major stock exchanges, the actual trade prices are constantly available to the public in many ways. The daily newspapers, of course, carry several pages of stock data, including, for all of the more active stocks, reports of the daily high, low, and closing prices, and the volume traded. Even in remote areas, papers often carry the daily closing prices and numbers of shares traded, and if the individual investor wants more information, there are ticker tapes and computers in all brokerage offices. Increasingly, we can all obtain up to the minute prices, either by a telephone call or with our own personal computers.

The bid and ask prices on the rare coin market are becoming more readily available to the public as well. In addition to the constant access of ANE and CCE members, publications such as *Coin World,* the *Greysheet,* and the *Bluesheet* regularly report coin prices.

The *Coin Dealer Newsletter,* or *Greysheet,* is "...a Monday morning report on the Coin Market" which is now in its 28th year of publication. It gives both bid and ask prices on most grades of raw or unslabbed coins, including type coins, coin sets, and BU rolls. In the past it has been very useful to coin collectors. However, the prices quoted may be higher or lower than the prices of actual trades on the ANE and the CCE, and dealers today use the *Greysheet* primarily for the pricing of BU rolls, proof sets, and mint sets.

The *Certified Coin Dealer Newsletter,* commonly called the *Bluesheet* because it is printed with blue ink, is, as the name implies, "a weekly report on the certified coin market." The editor states that the newsletter:

> uses every means available to insure accuracy and complete-ness of the bid prices shown. Since prices represent the highest known bids at press time and they are based strictly on dealer needs, prices will fluctuate according to these needs.

The *Bluesheet* reports bid prices only for all common grade (generally MS-61 through MS-67), Mint State and Proof coins certified by PCGS and NGC, and once each month, bid prices for a narrower range of ANACS and NCI-graded coins.

All certified coin values are based on ANE or CCE bids and asks.

Many investors are operating under the misconception that the *Bluesheet* is the basis for certified coin values. The truth is that the *Bluesheet* is only an indication of what bids are on the dealer-to-dealer computerized trading systems. The *Bluesheet* is not offering to buy or sell coins. When someone makes a cash offer for a coin (or anything else), that is a true indication of its value. And if you work with a reputable dealer, the offer he makes to buy your coins is based on the underlying bids on the computerized trading networks. Of course, if he is not a member dealer, his offer is based on what he can get when he sells to a member dealer.

For common date, generic coins, the spread between bid and ask prices is small. However, this is not true for truly rare, low population specimens. In addition, the prices of common date coins change rapidly. For these coins, the ANE and CCE pricing systems are very efficient, and the reporting of prices (for example, in the *Bluesheet*) normally is adequate to keep both dealers and their customers informed. However, the ANE and CCE bids on truly rare coins are only an indication of actual prices, and they seldom appear anywhere in print. Often actual transactions are much higher.

To illustrate this difference, not long ago the bid for a common date St. Gaudens $20 gold piece in Mint State 64 condition was $950 while the ask was $1,050—a 10% spread. At the same time, the first 1944-P Walking Liberty Half Dollar was certified in a Mint State 67 condition by PCGS. Since this was the first of these coins certified at this grade by either PCGS or NGC, there were no established trading prices on the Exchange. The *Bluesheet* arbitrarily assigned a bid price of $3,100, but the coin was actually acquired by a dealer for an asking price of $8,500. This appears to be a spread of 174% but, obviously, the published bid price was totally irrelevant to the coin's actual value.

You should be aware of the fact that a significant percentage of all coin transactions among dealers do not occur on the computerized trading networks but by private treaties. These occur when trades are made either by telephone or in person after private negotiations between dealers. This method of trading coins is a holdover from the time before the inception of the ANE or CCE. The existence and continued popularity of private treaties is a major obstacle in providing the public, or other dealers for that matter, with a published account of the latest coin trading prices.

Pricing information on certified coins has been, at times, difficult to pin down. As a result of the volatility that sometimes pervades the explosive rare coin market, various people in the industry have begun to create published price listings that, in various forms, provide dealers with bid, ask, and last trade prices for certified coins so they can make informed buying and selling decisions.

In November 1990 the publishers of the *Certified Coin Dealer Newsletter* started a new publication called the *CCDn Asksheet* which lists the lowest ask, or last trade, prices for certified coins. This publication may be relied upon by a dealer, in conjunction with other sources, as an indicator of truer current market values and price trends.

By the beginning of 1991, ANE is expected to begin reporting actual prices of dealer-to-dealer trades that take place on its exchange. This should help considerably to maintain a stable price structure for the more common date rare coins. However, the truly high-quality rarities will probably continue to be traded at auction or in private negotiations, not on the ANE or on the CCE. This is as it should be for, as we have suggested, coins that are extremely rare tend to be more like one-of-a-kind Old Master works of art than shares of stock and thus probably can never be traded as freely as most stocks.

The reader should understand that all bid and ask price reporting we have discussed, and actual trade prices reported by ANE and CCE, refer entirely to dealer-to-dealer trades, not to transactions with the public. This is different, and will continue to be different in the foreseeable future, from the reporting of securities transactions.

With securities, the actual dollars paid by a broker's client consist of the published price the securities firm must pay to acquire the stock plus a *commission* to the securities firm for handling the transaction. Commission rates on securities transactions are no longer regulated and can vary from one firm to another. However, the commission rate schedule used by any firm must be made known to the customer in advance. Actual commissions paid are calculated on a sliding scale based upon the price of the security and the number of shares purchased.

With rare coins, the total amount paid by a client consists of the ask (or a negotiated) price the dealer must pay to acquire the coin plus a *markup* to the dealer for processing the transaction. The markup added by a rare coin dealer, like the price actually paid for the coin, usually is not revealed to the customer. This is perfectly legitimate and in fact is no different from what happens when you buy an automobile, or furniture, or clothing. There are many reasons for applying different markup percentages from one item to another in any industry—most often reasons the consumer neither knows nor cares about—and the same thing is true in the rare coin industry.

The bottom line, however, is that in order to maximize your profit when you ultimately sell your rare coins, you must purchase them at prices that are fair and reasonable. How to accomplish this in a strange and unknown market is the major problem for most investors.

## IS THERE MANIPULATION IN THE MARKET?

Is there any manipulation in the pricing of rare coins? Yes! Some of it is legitimate and no different from what is found in the pricing of many other products—automobiles, for example—but unfortunately, there are also unscrupulous practices that the investor must protect against in order to make the big money we know is possible by investing in rare coins.

As an example of legitimate price manipulation, dealers frequently will attempt to control particular coin types or dates by buying heavily when prices are low. However, this is no different from buying heavily in a particular stock in order to acquire control or to force management to take some special action. Not long ago, for example, Carl Icahn bought a large, minority interest in USX Corporation for the expressed purpose of forcing management either to divest the company of its petroleum assets or by some other means to increase the value of the stock to the shareholders (and, incidentally, to himself). This is the type of action that you as a coin owner (or shareholder) want to see happen. It is what creates the big profits for you to enjoy.

However, there are also many high-pressure, dealer firms that regularly and systematically overcharge potential customers, either by conveying false grading and population data or by overpricing. As grading and population information becomes better understood, this kind of manipulation is increasingly more difficult to carry off. However, for the average investor it is much harder to avoid paying too much when you buy rare coins simply because it is hard to obtain the information necessary to protect yourself.

Here are some protective actions you can take:

1) Do everything you can to investigate and know your dealer. We emphasize this throughout this book, and it is *the* most important thing we can tell you. Once you have made a few trades you will know whether or not you are working with a dealer you can trust to treat you fairly. Even so, to maximize your profit, you should understand how the pricing system works and occasionally investigate the dealer prices and markups you are paying.

2) Dealer prices have been dealt with extensively in the earlier parts of this chapter. For most common date coins you can obtain an approximation of what a dealer would have to pay from publications such as the *Bluesheet*. But remember, always, that even with common date coins this is a relatively volatile market. What the *Bluesheet* says today can be quite different from what your dealer had to pay last week. The *Bluesheet* only publishes bid prices, what a dealer would like to pay for certain items. However, most transactions that actually take place are at the ask price or some compromise between the bid and the ask prices. For the more expensive rarities, there may be no way to know what your dealer paid. You just have to accept his price to you. However, you should not start out buying expensive rarities from any dealer. Get to know him or her first.

3) If you want to calculate the markup percentages you are paying to determine whether they are reasonable, the arithmetic is easy.

The following is an example of a $10,000 coin portfolio with a 20% markup:

---

Example:
    Wholesale cost of coins ....... $8,333
    With a markup of ................ $1,667
    Total retail cost .................. $10,000

---

What is "reasonable" is much more difficult. In a very general way, a markup from 15 to 25% from a respected dealer is fair and reasonable. On the purchase of a very expensive coin, though, a regular customer may pay considerably less than 15%. But we were recently told by a salesman that his firm regularly marks up coins as much as 700 to 800%, and there are many known cases of dealers customarily taking a profit of 100% or more on sales to customers. *Caveat emptor.*

4) The Consumer Numismatic Advisory Commission (CNAC) is a nonprofit rare coin consumer advocate organization that was created to protect investors against unethical dealer practices. CNAC will answer your inquiries by giving you a high and low price that a reputable dealer would charge for the coin in question, whether it is already in your portfolio or is a coin you are considering purchasing. See Appendix A.

5) Ask you dealer if he is trying to corner a particular coin or has a favorite coin type that he is pursuing. He may be manipulating a certain market by acquiring a select group of coins, which is perfectly legal. Don't be afraid to ask if there is something hot that he or she is working on. You may be able to get in on a good deal and make some money by being on the inside track.

To take advantage of the coin marketplace, learn as much as you can about how the pricing system works, and trade through a dealer who can make it work for you. This is the way professional coin traders and the secretive collector fraternity have been making their millions for many years.

# Chapter 7

# PUTTING IT ALL TOGETHER— HOW TO BUY AND SELL FOR MAXIMUM RETURN

In this chapter, we bring together the four classes of key players in the drama that has come to be called "the rare coin phenomenon":

1. The collectors
2. The coin dealers
3. The Wall Street brokerage firms
4. You, the individual investor

As we have said, our attempt with this book has been to provide you with a level playing field by pointing out the ways the other three groups have been able to profit from your lack of knowledge. How can you avoid this? How can you realize the potential profit that is rightfully yours by having invested in rare coins? That is what this chapter is about.

## YOU DON'T NEED A LOT OF MONEY TO MAKE A LOT OF MONEY

One of the biggest misconceptions that most people have about the rare coin market is that it takes a lot of money, that it is not very affordable. The truth is quality rare coins, the kind most of us should be considering for investment purposes, are more affordable than almost any other investment medium.

If one is considering an investment in art, for example, in order to buy a quality painting—say, a Rembrandt that someday in the future can probably be sold for a nice profit—it is necessary to invest large sums of money. Some people are constantly on the lookout for "undiscovered" painters in the hope that they can buy a relatively inexpensive painting that "someday" will increase in value. Most often such purchases are just that—a "hope" that the painter will be "discovered." The alternatives in the art world, though, are either to pay a great deal for a painting by a known master or to buy something cheap that may be pleasant to your tastes but will never be anything worthwhile as an investment.

It is possible to pay a great deal for a coin or a coin set—the King of Siam Set sold at auction in June 1990 for $2,900,000 plus a 10% buyer's commission, a new record high for a single auction lot transaction—but you can still buy a *high-quality* coin for $500 or less. It is an investment market that anyone can enter. In a short time, the average person, perhaps, will not be able to afford to buy high-quality/low population coins because the quantities are limited and, with the Wall Street firms acquiring coins as aggressively as they are, prices are bound to go higher. Yet today high-quality coins are still affordable.

We emphasized the term "high quality" in the paragraph above. We are often confronted with salespeople who point out how many more coins you could buy if you would lower your standards even slightly. They are right that lower quality coins sell for greatly reduced prices. But, it has been demonstrated over and over again that, for investment purposes—for the purpose of making money on the eventual sale of your coins—you should *always* buy the highest quality you can afford, even if it means acquiring fewer coins.

For example, if you are considering buying a Morgan dollar of common date, something that is not too expensive even in grades such as MS-65 or MS-66, and a salesman tries to convince you that you can buy, say, three of the same coins in grade MS-63 for the same amount of money, *always* go for the higher quality coin. If you are just collecting for your own enjoyment, then it is up to you, but if you want to make money, stay with the highest quality you can buy within your allotted coin budget.

This is a time of incredible investment opportunity. No matter what your age, whether you are in your 20s or in your 70s, buying high-quality rare coins is like buying money insurance. You purchase insurance to protect against the loss of your car, but the ravages of inflation and governmental legislation will do far more to destroy your earning ability at time of retirement than the complete loss of your car would cause. However much you have to invest, be it only enough for a single, good coin, do it. Make sure you have a good dealer, whose advice you value, and you are certain to make money over the long run. It may happen in six months that your dealer will suggest it is time to sell, to take your profit, but plan to leave your funds invested for several years for maximum profitability.

## HOW TO WORK WITH YOUR DEALER

In Chapter 3 we discussed the questions you should ask in selecting a dealer. Once you have decided upon the firm you want to use, you should learn as much as possible about how they do business, what they expect from you, and how you can best work together to accomplish your long-term profit objectives.

You probably will be working almost exclusively with one individual. In the beginning, you will talk with that man or woman frequently, in part as a get-acquainted process but also because he or she needs to know as much as possible about you if you are to be well served. Do not be offended if numerous questions are asked about your other investments, about your investment philosophy, your long-term financial goals, your tolerance for risk, and many other related matters.

Some investors are curious about how their funds are invested and will want to be informed any time there is any action in their account, even if they have given their dealer authority to act whenever it is believed to be in their best interest. Other investors are fearful, often expressing their fear as if it is a fear of losing their money when really they are afraid of making the big profits that are possible investing in rare coins.

The individual with whom you work has to know as much as

possible about you if you are to be well served. It helps a great deal, of course, if at some point in your dealings you have the opportunity to meet face to face. But even if this is not feasible, the more open you can be about your life, your family needs, and your financial affairs, the better it will be for you.

Once you reach the point where you are comfortable with both the firm and the person with whom you are dealing, tell that person anything that might have some bearing on your investing. Call them when there is any change, or when you have questions, and if they suggest you take a position when, for whatever reason, it isn't comfortable for you at that point in time, do not hesitate to say, "No, not now." Not only will they respect you for your honesty, they will also be able to make you a great deal more money over time if they know what your thoughts are and your tolerance for the inevitable swings in the market. Remember, coin prices do not move up or down within a dependable time frame. You must look at it from a long-term point of view, and not panic every time your investment moves 10 or 20%.

In other words, you must feel comfortable with your investment in rare coins, confident that your dealer will act at the proper time in your best interest. To accomplish this level of comfort, you must do your share. You must learn to know your dealer and to share with him or her anything that might have some bearing on how your affairs are handled. Your dealer representative is your friend. If you do not feel that friendship, get another person or go to another firm. But while he is still representing you, treat him as a friend, and work with him as a partner in building your wealth. You will be amazed at how much wealth such a partnership will generate for you if it is openly conceived and constantly nourished by friendly words and expressions of appreciation.

## WHICH COINS SHOULD YOU BUY—AND WHY

In most of the books on numismatics and rare coin investing, by the first or second chapter the reader is already confused by statements such as "Buy a Draped Bust" or "Buy a Liberty Seated Quarter," without knowing what these coins are. Probably most of us have seen a Morgan Silver Dollar or a St. Gaudens $20 gold piece but beyond these we're lost.

Many people are collectors by instinct and they make the mistake of thinking they have to collect some type or types of coins, or they have to collect a series—one coin type by date or by date and mint. In other words, they start out thinking that they want eventually to possess one of every Morgan Dollar that was ever minted. Many collectors work at putting together sets of coins, organized by pattern, by date, by coin type, or by mint mark. The ultimate collector, of course, is the person who is looking to have one of everything ever produced by the U.S. Mint. Not only is this almost impossible, even theoretically, it is absolutely not the best way to maximize your *investment* in rare coins.

The key to wise rare coin investing is to constantly look for quality. We would suggest avoiding foreign coins completely, primarily because they do not have the investment advantage of dependability that reliable grading has brought to the U.S. market (although it should be noted that PCGS is now grading some foreign coins). Foreign coins lack liquidity. Usually the strongest price for a foreign coin is in its country of origin.

Also, we would suggest avoiding copper coins as investment vehicles. A consideration when looking at copper coins is called "toning." A copper penny may be red, the original color; red brown, a partially toned coin; or brown, a coin having a full patina. Note that copper is an extremely active metal and carbon spots, which can severely diminish a coin's value, can develop even *after* encapsulation in a sonically-sealed slab.

In Appendix B you will find a complete, illustrated guide to *all* U.S. investment coins. Read the appropriate sections of this guide carefully whenever you are considering a new purchase, for it contains not just descriptions and pictures of coins but specific comments on the investment value of each coin type, with dates and grades to buy and to avoid in order to maximize your profits.

If you have sufficient confidence in your dealer to continue working with him or her, don't be overly concerned about what particular coin or coins you are buying. So long as they are Mint State or Proof and graded 64, 65, or better, with low populations, you can't go too far wrong.

Quality of coins means, first and foremost, coins that have been reliably graded as MS-64 or better. Don't let anyone tell you that you will come out ahead buying cheaper, lower grades of coins.

Have some diversification in your portfolio, and do not start out by buying a $50,000 ultra-rarity. This may be a great coin but it is a very thin market. Stick to U.S.-minted gold and silver coins of high grade, and trust your dealer to search out the specific coins that are underpriced at the time.

## HOW TO BORROW AGAINST YOUR COLLECTION

For one reason or another, everyone at times has a sudden need for extra cash. Perhaps it is April 13th and your accountant has just delivered your completed income tax return. You thought your quarterly payments had been sufficient but there was something you forgot about that increased your final tax payment substantially. Suddenly, you have that feeling of panic: "Where can I get some money—fast?"

Usually, one's first reaction is to think about going to your own bank for a personal loan. The idea of borrowing the money using your coins as collateral perhaps occurs to you, but the time involved in processing your loan application, through first the loan officer and then the bank's loan committee, seems to make this impractical. In addition, of course, you shudder to think of a rate of 4 to 6% over prime interest rate your local bank might exact from you if they finally did approve such a loan.

Financial emergencies always seem to occur at the very time when coin prices are low and you would rather be buying than selling. However, recognizing the security value of rare coins and the difficulty that coin investors can face at times such as these, several banks now provide what they call "asset-based" loans that can be processed very quickly. Using your coins as security, they make it possible for you to obtain needed funds the same day the application is signed. If one is located where the papers can be hand-carried to the bank, the money can be deposited to your account within a matter of hours.

In order to obtain a loan with rare coins as security, the coins must be delivered to the bank making the loan. Some of the larger dealers have arrangements with certain banks to provide funds for asset-based loans if the coins being held by the dealer as part of a managed account are deposited with the bank on behalf of the coins' owner. In such cases, the only thing that must be done is to obtain the signature of the borrower on the loan documents and the money can be wired to the borrower's account, even in another city. A good dealer, working with a bank, is sometimes able to obtain for his client a better borrowing rate—say, at the U.S. prime rate or at prime rate plus, perhaps, 2%— a far better interest rate than the customer could obtain if he were to borrow the cash from his own bank on a personal loan, or take an advance against his credit card.

It is advisable, at the time one is establishing a new account with a dealer, to inquire about the dealer's familiarity with borrowing procedures and rates, even if you have no immediate need for the funds at that time. The banks who will make such loans are located primarily in the major cities. When you get to more remote locations the bankers often have not even thought about lending money on rare coins. If they do set up an account for you it will be on the basis of your personal credit, not the value of the coins, and the interest rate will be several points higher than such an account established through a bank that gives out loans based upon certified rare coins.

Having an asset-based loan account established with your dealer's assistance will enable you to obtain funds with the same ease as borrowing on a margin account from your stockbroker. In both cases you receive favorable interest rates because the lender has virtually no risk of loss. After all, your assets are in their possession as long as the loan is outstanding, and it must be repaid before the coins (or stock) will be released to you.

## WHEN AND HOW TO SELL FOR MAXIMUM PROFIT

The one guarantee that a coin investor should insist upon from any dealer is that you have a lifetime buy-back guarantee, which means that at any time you choose to sell your coins, the company will buy them back from you at the absolute market prices—the then-current dealer bids. If a company is willing to give you this guarantee, you do not have to worry. Usually, if you are buying a coin of high quality/low population, graded by either PCGS or NGC, the company is going to be calling you back, offering you a profit long before you call them, wanting to sell.

The real question is: How much profit should you expect? And, of course, there is no exact answer to that question. In the stock market, there is a saying, "Bulls get rich and bears get rich, but hogs get slaughtered." Avoid at all costs, the temptation to develop a "Las Vegas" mentality, which is a way of thinking that says, "My coin has gone up 50 or 100% in a year; therefore, it will probably keep going up and I should never sell it."

It is our suggestion that you keep in mind the *double-up rule*: If you have doubled your money, take out your initial investment if you wish but leave the profit to be reinvested and keep reinvesting your profits. This is what turns a $5,000 or $10,000 or $15,000 portfolio into a $100,000 or $200,000 or $300,000 portfolio.

When to sell for maximum profit is something you may want to decide for yourself. However, if you have a managed portfolio with a reliable dealer, this is one of the decisions that the dealer will make for you. Even if you become a knowledgeable numismatist, you must recognize that the rare coin market can be extremely volatile. The right moment to respond to another dealer's bid on a particular coin some-times must be acted upon immediately or the moment is lost. Again, it comes down to trusting your dealer to act for you in a manner that will maximize your gains.

As you know, when you buy rare coins you pay a markup on the trade (this is what keeps the dealer in business). However, when you sell, many dealers credit your account with the full dealer bid price. In other words, if there is a bid price on the ANE or CCE computer, indicating that some dealer wants to buy it at that price, and your dealer thinks that it is time to sell, that bid price is what you will receive in your account.

With any investment, the decision as to when to sell is always hard. You want to maximize your profit, of course. But you know that if you get too greedy, you may end up defeating your own profit objectives. There is no secret that will guarantee that you can buy low and sell high. However, if you have purchased quality coins at times when market prices were favorable and you adhere to these few suggestions about selling, you *will* make a lot of money on your rare coin investment.

# Chapter **8**

# THE FIVE COMMANDMENTS FOR WEALTH BUILDING WITH COINS

Our purpose with this book is to provide an introduction to the subject of rare coin investing for any individual who may be somewhat less than an expert in the field. The book is designed with one purpose in mind: to teach you how to be a successful coin *investor*.

The word "investor" is emphasized so you will not think of this as merely another book on coin *collecting*. The distinction is important. A successful coin investor may also be a collector of coins, but your primary objective as an investor always will be to create wealth for yourself and your family.

Investing in rare coins is definitely one very important means by which the objective of building wealth can be accomplished. Still, as with any investment, there are potential pitfalls. To be a *successful* rare coin investor you must discipline yourself to avoid these pitfalls. To accomplish this, we have labeled this chapter, "The Five *Commandments* for Wealth Building ..." Learn them well. Follow them *always* and you *will* be successful in building wealth with rare coins.

The five commandments are:
- Buy only slabbed coins
- Buy only coins graded by PCGS or NGC
- Buy only high-quality coins
- Know your dealer—work with him or her as a partner
- Consult the Consumer Numismatic Advisory Commission

## BUY ONLY SLABBED COINS

The experienced numismatist is able to examine any coin and give an immediate opinion of 1) whether the coin is genuine or a counterfeit; 2) whether it has been whizzed or by other means refurbished in an attempt to make it appear to be of higher quality than it is; and 3) the probable grade that should be assigned according to the American Numismatic Association Grading Scale (Figures 4 and 5). These are all subjective evaluations, but there is a surprising unanimity among different experts when they examine a particular coin. Often these opinions can be obtained simply by examination by the naked eye or with a hand-held magnifying glass.

The various grading services in most cases (not all) summarize the opinions of their in-house experts and then sonically seal the coin under examination in a plastic container, along with the serial number they have assigned that coin and the grade they have given to it. These containers are tamper-proof, and a prospective buyer of a coin sealed in one of these containers or "slabs" (thus the derivation of the phrase "a slabbed coin") can be sure that the coin is genuine and that it has not been physically changed since leaving the mint, other than through normal bag marks and circulation wear.

It is extremely important that an investor *always* buy slabbed coins unless he is sufficiently skilled as a numismatist to determine authenticity and grading himself. There is probably no field where the expression "A little bit of knowledge is a dangerous thing" fits more accurately than in buying rare coins. Even the experts are sometimes fooled. The moderately well-informed investor will often make mistakes in judging the authenticity and grading of a coin.

Even though you may occasionally miss out on great wealth by not buying that "bargain" coin you see at a garage sale or a flea market, your long-term investment program will produce much greater wealth if you just refuse to buy any coin that is not slabbed.

## BUY ONLY COINS GRADED BY PCGS OR NGC

As we have explained in Chapter 4, not all grading services are equal. Some of them, such as ANACS, do a superior job of authenticating the validity of a coin, but their grading has been questioned by many dealers. Other grading services are suspect because they grade coins too high, specifically to provide a dealer with an excuse to tell a prospective buyer, "This is a graded coin," without revealing the firm that did the grading.

Any coin graded and slabbed by the Professional Coin Grading Service (PCGS) or the Numismatic Guaranty Corporation of America (NGC) can be purchased or sold on the American Numismatic Exchange (ANE) or the Certified Coin Exchange (CCE) sight unseen. Thus, you can buy any PCGS or NGC-graded coin, and no others, with the full assurance that the coin is authentic and that the assigned grade will be accepted by any dealer anywhere in the United States.

With any purchase you are contemplating, do not ask just the grade of the coin, but also the firm that has done the grading. Protect your investment from the beginning. Buy only coins graded by PCGS or NGC!

## BUY ONLY HIGH-QUALITY COINS

What is high quality? There may be some exceptions for extremely rare coins, where very few or no mint state or proof specimens are known to exist, but as a general rule, we would say that high quality in silver or nickel coins mean Mint State or Proof coins graded 65 or above, and high quality in gold coins means Mint State or Proof coins graded 64 or above. We do not recommend buying copper coins for investment purposes.

In addition to the grades of the coins you buy, we also suggest that you buy the coins with dates and mint marks that the PCGS and NGC Population Reports show having relatively low populations. We say "relatively low" because the coins that are true rarities, with populations of, perhaps, five or less, usually are very expensive. Thus, it is a matter of compromise for most people. But you should always place your investment dollars in the lowest population coins that you can afford, even if it means that you will have a smaller number of coins in your portfolio than you would if you bought more populous and less expensive coins.

Quality, quality, quality—it will always build your wealth faster, and more dependably, than buying larger numbers of lower quality coins.

## KNOW YOUR DEALER—WORK WITH HIM OR HER AS A PARTNER

In this book we have dealt at length with the related problems of selecting the right dealer and how to work with the dealer you select. It is not necessary to elaborate on this further, except to point out some of the damaging consequences that can come from dealing with firms you have not investigated sufficiently.

If you have determined to religiously follow the first three commandments we have recommended, you will undoubtedly obtain investment-quality coins. However, there are thousands of cases of quality coins being purchased at *grossly inflated prices.* Even some large, well-advertised dealers regularly make a practice of selling coins with markups in excess of 100% over prevailing bid prices. When coins are purchased at prices such as these, their investment value is greatly diminished.

*Know your dealer!* Find someone you can trust and stay with them. Do not move around looking for a better price each time you buy something. There is no way the average investor can stay on top of the constantly fluctuating market. You must find a dealer who will do this for you.

## CONSULT THE CONSUMER NUMISMATIC ADVISORY COMMISSION

CNAC provides its members with an investor-oriented, quarterly update on the rare coin market, and nonpartisan, written price quotations (minimum and maximum) on any U.S. coins, whether owned by the member or being contemplated for purchase.

The organization was created by a grant from a dealer who was concerned about the many instances of consumers not knowing all of the ins and outs of the coin business and, as a result, purchasing fraudulent coins, improperly graded coins, or overpriced coins.

This is strictly a consumer group. In fact, dealers, wholesalers, or anyone else connected with the coin industry are not allowed to be members.

As this is being written, CNAC is relatively new. It is described in Appendix A. We strongly encourage you to become a part of it and to support it, not only for your own protection but also for the protection of those who may be interested in purchasing your coins in the future.

# Chapter 9

# WHAT YOU CAN EXPECT IN THE NEXT DECADE

The evolution of the rare coin market has been tremendous since the early 1960s. The *Red Book* (R.S. Yeoman: *A Guide Book of United States Coins*) was the most popular pricing instrument in the late 50s and early 60s, along with monthly coin magazines (where one could advertise to buy or sell), various dealers' price lists, coin shows, and auctions. The *Red Book* was the main instrument, however, and a dealer, upon receiving his new yearly issue, would check over his inventory to bring his prices up to the *Red Book* level. Getting a copy early was a tremendous advantage. You could travel from coin shop to coin shop and pick up all the underpriced items. Lack of communication was the main problem. It was not unusual for an item to be $6 on the West Coast, $5 on the East Coast, and $4 in the Midwest.

The actual original distribution of the coins determined how common or scarce they might be in a particular area. With poor communications and an uneven distribution system coins were inclined to be priced more by availability than actual scarcity.

The next step in the evolution was the weekly coin newspapers. Now dealers across the country could advertise their inventory or their new higher buy prices. Prices could actually change on a weekly basis, a tremendous step up in the industry. The uneven distribution of collectors' coins now started to even out. Most of the "S" mint coins were on the West Coast. Midwest and Eastern collectors could now order these coins and plug them into the holes in their coin boards.

The third step, that seemed like the ultimate, was the formation of a teletype system. The first system was the United States Coin Exchange, out of Detroit. A nucleus of 25 dealers from across the nation could type their various buys and sells live on the teletype. We could now have instantaneous price changes. Of course, the equipment was far from state-of-the-art. The lines were run across old Western Union lines and old Western Union teletype equipment was used. Any major rain storm would bring the lines down. Actually there was probably more down time than on-line time. The teletypes themselves were old discarded equipment and full-time servicemen were kept busy keeping the equipment patched together. Despite the line and equipment problem there were more important problems: the coins themselves.

Price changes meant nothing when the coin grading was not universal. Grading was a subjective art and coins went winging back and forth through the mail to be either accepted or rejected by the various buyers. This is where things bogged down. Except for vast improvements in the teletype wire services and a large growth in the membership of participating dealers nothing else was evolving. Competing teletype systems emerged and the equipment and systems improved with the competition.

The only significant step forward was the starting of the ANACS certification and subsequently the ANACS grading service. These certified and graded coins traded for some years with some consumer confidence, but they still required sight acceptance by the various dealers, and customer approval could take a week or more to complete a transaction. The lull between the birth of ANACS and any new improvements was a long one. Finally, in 1986, the Professional Coin Grading Service (PCGS) was founded and things have changed very rapidly since then.

What will be the most important developments in the rare coin industry over the next decade? No one knows for sure, but David Hall, president of PCGS, is in as good a position as anyone to venture a guess. We agree with the statements expressed in his newsletter, *Inside View,*

January 1990.

The rare coin market is headed down a very specific path. The two major components of the path are computer technology and financial institution participation. The positive aspects of this future path are monumental increases in marketplace efficiency, liquidity, safety, and available information, and a drastic reduction in dealer profit margins. The one negative aspect is a significant increase in price volatility.

The rare coin market of 1990 is dramatically different from the rare coin market of 1980, but the rare coin market of 2000 will be virtually unrecognizable. We are facing a decade of monumental, mostly positive change. There were 10 significant events in the 1980s, in the 1990s there most likely will be 20 or 30 or more!

At this stage it is a little bit of guesswork since the market is sailing in uncharted waters, but the focus of the next decade's significant events should be in four areas: Wall Street, computer grading, new trading methods and auxiliary services, and, of course, price milestones.

## INCREASED WALL STREET INVOLVEMENT

Wall Street is involved in the numismatic marketplace. That's a simple, undeniable fact. This involvement will probably continue to evolve in four areas:

First, there will be more "funds," some of them designed to buy and hold rare coins for the life of the fund, others designed to be trading partnerships, and perhaps others with other objectives. Besides the Kidder Peabody Fund, we will probably see several more funds in the 1990s. And the numbers will get bigger. Already in 1990, a $100,000,000 fund has been announced.

Second, we're going to see Wall Street firms involved directly in the retail marketing of rare coins. They already sell Gold Eagles and other bullion coins and they have recently started to sell individual numismatic coins, such as PCGS-graded $20 St. Gaudens, through their retail outlets.

Third, we'll undoubtedly see many more mergers and acquisitions. Don't be surprised if some of the coin market's major firms cut deals with large corporations and conglomerates. The purchase of Blanchard by General Electric is just the beginning.

Finally, we should see some significant Initial Public Offerings (IPOs) coming out of the numismatic industry. One day soon you may turn on "Wall Street Week" and hear Martin Zweig say, "I like XYZ Coin Company, trading over-the-counter as COIN. They have a 12% share of the exotic coin market."

## COMPUTER GRADING

The importance of objective coin grading cannot be overstated. As technology evolves in the areas of computer hardware and software it is inevitable that expert systems will be developed that can quickly and accurately grade coins in the most consistent, unbiased way possible. As we have already mentioned, PCGS uses a computer system to grade coins. By the time you are reading this, it is more than likely that NGC will also be using a computer grading process.

Nobody can say as of this date how coin grading will evolve over the next few years, but based on recent changes and with ever-increasing technology, we have no doubt that such changes will provide investors with an even more precise way of knowing that the coins that they invest in are of the highest quality due to more objective grading.

## MANY NEW TRADING METHODS

Now let's talk about new trading methods and all the possible auxiliary services. Focus on the current direction of the coin market and let your imagination run wild. You may see a future that includes storage facilities—giant coin warehouses. You may see an actual exchange that clears coin trades—a central clearinghouse. You may see a fast and efficient way to borrow money using coins as collateral—margin transactions. You may see futures contracts on the most frequently traded, bullion related coins—maybe even an index based on a basket of coins. Not only is all of this possible—it will probably all happen during the next 10 years.

## PRICES

Finally, we must talk about coin prices. Simply put, the next decade will see geometric price milestones. The 1980s saw the first $1,000,000 coin; the 1990s will see the first $10,000,000 coin. We're due for two massive bull markets and one major bear market in the next decade. It's going to be a wild and exciting ride. And, if you are patient and careful, it should be enormously profitable for you.

For rare coins, the 1960s were a decade of unbridled speculation; the 1970s were a decade of rampant inflation; and the 1980s were a decade of revolutionary market changes. The 1990s will be a decade of massive growth—and the numbers will be nearly beyond imagination.

## THE FUTURE

We have talked about a $10,000,000 coin and the possibility of futures contracts on coin exchanges. Comparing coins prices from 1980 to 1990, some coins went up over 7900%! (See the October 1990 Coin Dealer Newsletter.) The facts are self-evident. Opportunity is knocking and that window of opportunity can come slamming down at any moment. Do you want to be on the inside reaping incredible profits or on the outside looking in? The choice is yours. Make a move now. Take a stance. Don't be a bystander, be a winner. It is not a question of money but one of time. Can you afford not to? The answer is obvious.

# Postscript

If you have enjoyed and profited from reading this book, you will certainly want to know about two future publications that will be forthcoming from Chicago Financial Publications, Inc.

The first is another book that will contain all of the information needed for you to become a skilled numismatist: how to examine a coin; the peculiarities of different coin types and varieties; how to grade coins yourself; the special circumstances to look for in searching out sleepers; what to look for in determining whether or not a coin is a counterfeit or has been altered; and more.

The second publication is to be a comprehensive series of video tapes, organized into a complete course on numismatics. With this series of tapes, you will actually be looking at a wide variety of coins from many different, close-up angles, while the authors call your attention to all of the important items that you need to observe in order to understand the finer nuances of grading and any other matter that might help you determine the real value, as well as the probable price, of any particular coin.

Both of these will be available from the same source where you bought this book, sometime in the spring of 1991.

# Appendix **A**

## THE CONSUMER NUMISMATIC ADVISORY COMMISSION

The Consumer Numismatic Advisory Commission, Inc. (CNAC) is a nonprofit consumer organization created to protect investors against gross overpricing and other unscrupulous activities practiced by some coin companies. Coin dealers, coin shops, and coin wholesalers are not allowed to become members.

Currently, rare coins are the last unregulated investment available to the general public. Coins may be bought and sold from a dealer without filling out any forms and without revealing your social security number or even your name if you should so desire. The dealer is not required to file 1099 forms with the IRS (except for cash transactions over $10,000), nor to reveal any other information about the transactions in which his clients engage.

However, some coin companies are taking advantage of this freedom from regulation to engage in a wide variety of schemes to fleece the public. As just one example, there is a company in Arizona that is selling silver American Eagles for $80, which is a 900% markup on their cost of $8. And, to add to the seriousness of their crime (which is truly what it is), they have an added pyramid-scheme "incentive" under which each customer who signs someone else up to buy eight or more receives a $10 cash bonus. There are a number of such scams occurring today.

The organizers of CNAC are convinced that these dealers who are taking advantage of the naïveté of new coin investors can best be controlled through self-regulation. The alternative will be to wait until consumer complaints lead the government to intervene, with solutions that will restrict the entire industry.

Some form of control is clearly needed. CNAC is an attempt to provide this from within, in order to protect us all from federal regulation and, possibly, new legislation that would require the reporting and taxation of individual coin transactions. CNAC has only one goal: internal regulation of the coin market by providing the consumer with a source of accurate, unbiased information and current prices.

CNAC will give you high and low price parameters so that you can ascertain whether the price you are paying (or have paid) is reasonable. In addition, CNAC will tell you the population of the coin and give you a brief appraisal of the coin's projected potential for appreciation.

CNAC is a newly formed, long overdue organization that has a primary goal of protecting and advising the consumer and is still solidifying the services that it intends to provide. But contact them to find out what's going on.

CNAC is located at 325 Pennsylvania Avenue, SE, Washington, DC 20003. Call them at 202-675-6370 if you would like more information.

# Appendix **B**

## AN ILLUSTRATED GUIDE TO U.S. COINS

On the following pages you will find descriptions of most United States coin types, together with photographs and detailed comments. Some types are (or are not) recommended for their probable long-term investment value. For those that are recommended, the best dates or condition grades are clearly indicated.

Detailed descriptions of known varieties and the numbers of each coin originally minted will be found in the *Red Book* (R.S. Yeoman: *A Guide Book of United States Coins*, 43rd Edition, 1990). The PCGS and NGC Population Reports should be consulted for quantities certified to date.

# COPPER COINS
## Half Cent (1793–1857)

The case against half cents is that they are made out of copper. We do not recommend copper coins as long-term investments. Copper is an active metal and even if "slabbed" it can "grow" carbon spots that will severely diminish its value.

## Large Cent (1793–1857)

The backbone of U.S. coin collecting in the early 19th century. Not recommended for investment.

## Flying Eagle and Indian Cent (1857–1909)

There are some rarities and beautiful coins in this series in both proof and mint state. These coins should, however, be left to the collector. Their investment record is very poor.

**Lincoln Cent (1909–Present)**

A collector series. Little or no potential for the serious investor.

**Two Cent Piece (1864–1873)**

Few have survived in full mint red. Few proofs have survived unhairlined and in full color because they are copper. Not recommended for investment.

# NICKEL COINS
## Three Cent Nickel (1865–1889)

The three cent denomination was very important in 1865—it cost three cents to mail a letter. The Three Cent Nickel was introduced to replace the Three Cent Silver (too small) and the extremely unpopular Three Cent Fractional Note, which became very ragged with over-use.

The Three Cent Nickel is one our favorite coins, especially proofs. High-grade proofs have spectacular eye appeal. Some exquisite examples have deeply mirrored fields with cameo devices and have fire and sparkle reminiscent of gemstones. We recommend all dates of Three Cent Nickels in Proof-65 and strongly recommend Proof-66 and higher.

Mint state Three Cent Nickels can also exhibit a lot of pizzazz, and they are very elusive in high grades. We recommend them in MS-64 (except for the first year of issue, 1865, which is too common) and all dates are recommended in MS-65 and higher. Avoid coins with carbon spots.

**Shield Nickel (1866–1883)**

There are two basic varieties: the "with rays" reverse of 1866 and 1867, and the "no rays" reverse 1867–1883. The latter type is recommended for larger portfolios in Mint State and Proof-65 or better. The rare rays type is only recommended for large portfolios, also in Mint State and Proof-65 or better. Again, watch for carbon spots.

**Liberty Nickel (1883–1912)**

Two varieties: "with" and "no cents." Recommended only in Proof-66 or better. Both varieties are recommended. Expect to pay about 35% more for the without cents variety. As with all nickel coins avoid carbon spots.

**Buffalo Nickel (1913–1938)**

Selected dates in Mint State-65 are currently underpriced and should be affordable for even the smallest portfolios. Brilliant proofs, issued only in 1936 and 1937, are highly recommended in Proof-66 or better. The early Matte Proof Buffaloes from 1913 to 1916 are best left to the specialist as they lack the liquidity so important in today's market.

**Jefferson Nickel (1938–Present)**

The series is too modern for consideration. The exception is the 1942-P proof silver nickel. The silver nickels were issued only from 1942–1945 because nickel became a critical war material. The 1942-P is the only silver nickel ever struck in proof. Recommended in Proof-66.

## SILVER COINS
### Three Cent Silver, Types I, II and III (1851–1873)

There were three basic designs over the 23 years this series was issued. Type I should be considered for investment in MS-65; Type II in MS-65 and also the very rare Type II proofs in 64 and 65. Type III is recommended in MS-65 and Proof-65.

### Flowing Hair Half Dime (1794–1795)

The price of these in investment quality is prohibitive except for the largest portfolios.

**Draped Bust Half Dime, Small Eagle (1796–1797)**

There are better places to put your money for what it would cost to secure these in MS-63 or better.

**Draped Bust Half Dime, Heraldic Eagle (1800–1805)**

Beyond the reach of most portfolios in the grade we would recommend.

## Capped Bust Half Dime (1829–1837)

A mild recommendation in Mint State 64, Mint State 65 and up is okay for large portfolios.

## Liberty Seated Half Dime, No Stars (1837–1838)

This two year type is in great demand by serious type collectors. Prohibitively rare in proof. Recommended in Mint State 64 or better.

**Liberty Seated Half Dime, With Stars (1838–1859)**

Although investors often shun small coins, some extremely rare proofs from 1838 to 1853 occasionally appear on the market at reasonable prices. These should be considered for larger and longer term portfolios. Most of the readily available proofs are dated 1858 and 1859 and we would avoid these. Earlier date Mint State 64 or better pieces are recommended for long term investment.

**Liberty Seated Half Dime, With Arrows (1853–1855)**

This is a short series but not in great demand. Not recommended for the average portfolio.

**Liberty Seated Half Dime, Legend Obverse (1860–1873)**

Suitable for medium size portfolios in Mint State and Proof 65 or better. Again, not highly recommended because of the coin size. Buy scarcer date Proof and Mint State pieces when available at small premiums to common dates.

**Draped Bust Dime, Small Eagle (1796–1797)**

Rare and for the advanced collector.

## Draped Bust Dime, Heraldic Eagle (1798–1807)

Far too expensive in investment quality except for the largest portfolios.

## Capped Bust Dime, Large Size (1809–1828)

Too expensive except for the largest portfolios.

**Capped Bust Dime, Small Size (1828–1837)**

Could be considered in Mint State 64 for a portfolio large enough to absorb it.

**Liberty Seated Dime, No Stars (1837–1838)**

We like this two year type because of strong collector demand, rarity, and attractiveness. Recommended in Mint State 64 and better. Proofs are excessively rare and of the survivors a large percentage are mishandled.

**Liberty Seated Dime, With Stars (1838–1860)**

A mild recommendation in Mint State 65 or better. High-quality proofs should be considered for larger and long-term portfolios.

**Liberty Seated Dime, With Arrows (1853–1855)**

This is a short series but the mintages and survival rates are fairly high enough to keep type collectors supplied. Proofs are rare. There are better places to put your funds.

**Liberty Seated Dime, Legend (1860–1891)**

A long series with many common dates in both proof and mint state to continuously supply collector demand. Not commonly collected by date in mint state or proof. Mild recommendation in Mint State and Proof 65 or better, but there are many better places to put your money.

**Liberty Seated Dime, With Arrows (1873–1874)**

Unlike the earlier 1853 arrows variety, this short series is actively sought by collectors and investors. Recommended in Mint State and Proof 64 or better.

**Barber Dime (1892–1916)**

A very long series but actively collected in both mint state and proof by collectors. Without discussing individual dates (many are very scarce), we recommend these in Mint State and Proof 66 or better. As with the Liberty Seated Dime With Legend, buy scarcer Mint State coins any time the premium is small.

**Mercury Dime (1916–1945)**

There are some truly rare and scarce mint state dates in this series but generally we would avoid these as investments. Beware of the later dates in "wonder grades" (67–68) at high prices. There is a tremendous overhanging supply, including bag quantities, that could quickly crush price levels if they reach the certification services. 1936–1942 proofs are highly recommended in 67. The proof mintages are low to begin with and few have survived or ever were struck as Proof-67.

**Twenty Cent Piece (1875–1878)**

All but one piece (1876-CC) is obtainable in mint state or proof. We like these short popular series and so do collectors and investors. Recommended in Mint State and Proof 64 or better. Two proof only dates, 1877 and 1878, can often be purchased at small premiums. Buy these on those occasions.

**Draped Bust Quarter, Small Eagle (1796)**

An extremely popular one year type coin. We do not recommend this for investment as we consider it fully priced.

**Draped Bust Quarter, Heraldic Eagle (1804–1807)**

Not recommended for most portfolios because of the high cost. The rare 1804 could be considered as an investment in almost any grade but caution is suggested as many have been damaged and repaired.

**Capped Bust Quarter, Large Size (1815–1828)**

Although rare in high grade this series is not recommended for most portfolios because of the high cost and limited demand.

## Capped Bust Quarter, Small Size (1831–1838)

Pristine pieces with good eye appeal can be considered for those with large portfolios.

## Liberty Seated Quarter, No Motto (1838–1866)

A long series with many dates in both mint state and proof. It is difficult to make general comments and to ignore specific date and mint mark combinations. The demand for quality mint state or proof types is strong. Buy quality Mint State and Proof types. Date selection using mintage figures in combination with population reports can garner some sleepers.

## Liberty Seated Quarter, Arrows and Rays (1853)

Very scarce and in demand. Difficult to find even in the higher circulated grades. If you can obtain a quality mint state piece near the current quoted market price it is an excellent long-term hold.

## Liberty Seated Quarter, Arrows, No Rays (1854–1855)

Although scarce, not nearly as sought after as the previous variety. Recommended only if available at the right price.

**Liberty Seated Quarter, With Motto (1866–1891)**

We like these in extremely high-quality mint state or proof. We especially like the rare dates 1879 to 1890 in high-quality mint state, because of collector demand.

**Liberty Seated Quarter, With Arrows (1873–1874)**

A very popular two year type coin recommended in either mint state or proof. the mint state prices look especially attractive right now. Many proofs have been harshly cleaned or mishandled. Buy in Mint State or Proof 64 or better.

**Barber Quarter (1892–1916)**

As with the Barber Dime series, the quarters are widely favored by collectors in mint state and proof. We like the common dates in Mint State or Proof 66 and up, and the scarce dates in Mint State 65 and up.

**Standing Liberty Quarter Type I (1916–1917)**

The 1916 is very rare in any condition and is a favorite and in great demand by date collectors. It should be considered for investment in high quality mint state. The 1917 is a favorite with Type coin collectors as almost all 1917s come fully struck with a full head. The 1917 coins however are not currently recommended for investment.

**Standing Liberty Quarter Type II (1917–1930)**

We have a few favorite dates in this type. Selected dates should be considered during price rollbacks.

**Washington Quarter (1932–Present)**

A long, boring series, far too modern and overpromoted. There are many more early rolls overhanging the market than demand can consume for a long time to come. Although high-quality proofs are quite expensive, demand is slim and we don't recommend them.

## Flowing Hair Half Dollar (1794–1795)

The price of this type is out of range for most investors in the quality we would recommend.

## Draped Bust Half Dollar, Small Eagle (1796–1797)

Excessively rare.

**Draped Bust Half Dollar, Heraldic Eagle (1801–1807)**

In the quality necessary for investment, out of range for most portfolios.

**Capped Bust Half Dollar, Lettered Edge (1807–1836)**

These have performed very well in Mint State 64 and better. Avidly collected by date and by every variety and overdate available.

## Capped Bust Half Dollar, Reeded Edge (1836–1839)

A very short series that enjoys good collector and investor demand. These are fine in high quality for larger portfolios.

## Liberty Seated Half Dollar, No Motto (1839–1866)

Many varieties and rare dates are available including a good number of sleepers. A popular and elusive type in high-quality mint state or proof. Recommended.

## Liberty Seated Half Dollar, Arrows and Rays (1853)

Very difficult to find high quality specimens appropriately priced, but still well worth the investment, especially for long-term large portfolios.

## Liberty Seated Half Dollar, Arrows, No Rays (1854–1855)

A two year type with good collector demand. Recommended in high quality for large portfolios.

**Liberty Seated Half Dollar, With Motto (1866–1891)**

Popular and in demand in both proof and mint state. We especially like the scarce dates 1879–1890 in Mint State 65 or better. These enjoy more collector demand than the same dates of the Liberty Seated Quarters previously mentioned. Almost anything in high quality is good for investment in either mint state or proof.

**Liberty Seated Half Dollar, With Arrows (1873–1874)**

A short series that is in demand and very elusive in high quality proof or mint state. The Proof 65 halves are especially tough. Recommended in either Mint State or Proof 64 or better.

**Barber Half Dollar (1892–1915)**

    A popular series with collectors and investors alike. Although it is a long series it has no stoppers in either proof or mint state. Collected in mint state by date and mint mark. Collected in proof by date. Spectacular high grade examples are occasionally available on the market in both proof and mint state. These are highly recommended and should be acquired if at all possible. They have a great long-term potential. There are many sleepers to be ferreted out of the mint state series. These "finds" could produce tremendous profits in the next few years. The population reports help reveal their true scarcity.

**Walking Liberty Half Dollar (1916–1947)**

    Considered one of the most beautiful U.S. coins, the Walking Liberty Half Dollar enjoys strong collector demand. This is another series where you should ignore mintages and apply the knowledge of just how nice each date and mint mark combination was initially struck, and how many have survived.

Common dates in Mint State 65 and even some Mint State 66 should not be held for long term but only for market-related, short-term plays. There are some original $1,000 bags and many original rolls of common date Walkers being held off the market. Consult a knowledgeable dealer familiar with Walking Halves for specific date, mint, and quality recommendations.

Proof Walkers, issued only from 1936 to 1942, are highly recommended. The 1936 in Proof 65, the 1937 to 1941 in Proof 66 or 67, if they fit into your portfolio, and the 1942 in Proof 67. Using these grades as criteria, your pieces will rank among the finest known from a series whose mintage is slim to begin with.

### Franklin Half Dollar (1948–1963)

Far too modern for consideration. Don't even consider the late date wonder-grade coins.

### Flowing Hair Silver Dollar (1794–1795)

A two year type with the 1794 being one of the classic rarities of American numismatics. In high quality these are expensive and out of range of all but the largest portfolios. Even the more common 1795 is prohibitively costly in high grade.

**Draped Bust Silver Dollar, Small Eagle (1795–1798)**

As above, not in the price range of most portfolios.

**Draped Bust Silver Dollar, Heraldic Eagle (1798–1803)**

A good long-term investment in mint state for those with large holdings.

**Gobrecht Silver Dollar (1836–1837)**

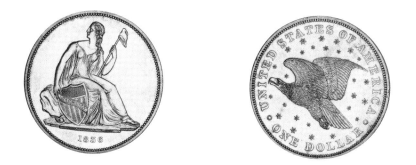

Issued in an attempt to resume coinage of the United States dollars. Low mintage. Many are patterns and restrikes issued to meet collector demand. Best left to the collector and type specialist. In high quality they are out of the price range of most investors.

## Liberty Seated Silver Dollar (1840–1873)

Two varieties: No Motto 1840-1865 and With Motto 1866-1873. The No Motto is the scarcer of the two. Although there are many rare dates in both mint state and proof, we don't think this series will ever have enough demand by date collectors. As type coins still recommended in high quality for larger portfolios.

**Trade Dollar (1873–1885)**

Popular and a good item for potential profit in Proof and Mint State 63 or better. Select the best you can afford for your portfolio.

**Morgan Dollar (1878–1921)**

This is a series of coins that, for the most part, was not collected until the mid-1960s. They were readily available in the banks in mint condition, and the Treasury also had a hoard. The release of the Treasury-held dollars, plus the discovery of the great "Redfield Hoard," gave tremendous publicity to the collecting of silver dollars and, within a few years, they became the most sought after coin series of all. This demand has not waned and the Morgan Dollar is still the king of U.S. coins.

A dealer who has been active in the business for 15 or more years has a big step up on any newer dealer or investor just entering the dollar market. The years of experience, noting just what date and mint mark dollars appeared in quantity, the knowledge that certain dollars seldom come well-struck, etc., added to the current population figures of certified coins, help the knowledgeable dealer better select the winners from the long list of dollars available. And winners there are.

Many dollars, after all these years of collecting and investing, are still tremendously underpriced, especially proof-like and deep mirror proof-like examples. That is why it is imperative that you work with a vendor who has solid market knowledge to select the date, mint mark, and condition of the dollars in which you invest. This is not written to discourage you from investing in dollars, because you should, but to encourage you to use professional help in your selection.

A few "don'ts": Don't buy uncertified Morgan Dollars at bargain prices. One point on the grading scale can mean the difference of hundreds or even thousands of dollars in value. Don't buy BU rolls of silver dollars. The quality coins from these rolls have long since been picked out, leaving the low-end, nonperforming coins. Don't buy low-grade Morgan Dollars—they are common and not in demand. Don't buy common date dollars, even high-quality certified ones, unless you are knowingly making a short-term play to take advantage of a market opportunity. Money can be made on these price moves but they are a terrible long-term hold.

Proof Morgan Dollars are recommended in grade 64 or better.

**Peace Dollar (1921–1935)**

Although Peace Dollars are not sought after like Morgan Dollars, they are still quite popular. It is reasonably easy to assemble a complete set and so they are widely collected. There are many dates that are underpriced. This series is still gaining popularity, and is another series where you should consult an experienced dealer when making selections for investment purposes. As always, quality is very important.

# GOLD COINS
## Gold Dollar Type I, Liberty Head (1849–1854)

Good long-term potential in Mint State 64 or better. Excessively rare in proof. Date consideration is not of great importance except for long-term holds.

## Gold Dollar Type II, Indian Head (1854–1856)

This has always been one of our favorite coins. Issued for just three years with only two dates (1854-P and 1855-P) being within range of most investors. The series enjoys great demand from gold type collectors. Even the 1854 and 1855 dates are very scarce in mint state and are truly rare in high quality. Strongly recommended in Mint State 64 or better for larger portfolios. Few proofs exist.

**Gold Dollar Type III, Indian Head (1856–1889)**

Although this is a long series most of the available mint state pieces fall within a few dates. We would recommend these in Mint State 64 or better and suggest you select low mintage dates. They are occasionally available at a modest premium above the common dates. Also recommended in Proof 64 and up when low population pieces (25–50) are available.

**Quarter Eagle, Capped Bust to Right (1796–1807)**

All are rare in mint state and beyond the means of most investors.

**Quarter Eagle, Large Capped Bust to Left (1808)**

A one year type that is excessively rare in mint state.

## Quarter Eagle, Small Capped Bust to Left (1821–1834)

All mintages are 6,000 pieces or less and thus very rare in high-quality mint state.

## Quarter Eagle, Classic Head (1834–1839)

Truly scarce in mint state. We like this type, any date, in Mint State 63 or better for large portfolios.

## Quarter Eagle, Liberty (1840–1907)

This coin is very popular with gold type collectors and common dates are recommended in Mint State 65 or better if purchased during a market pull back. There are many low mintage dates that are recommended in Mint State 64 or better. Wise date selection can greatly enhance the profit potential of this series. Proofs are occasionally bargain priced and recommended in Proof 64 or better, especially low mintage pieces.

## Quarter Eagle, Indian (1908–1929)

By far the most popular series of gold one can expect to complete as an entire date and mint mark collection. It enjoys great demand from collectors and investors. Far too many of these have survived in mint state to recommend it in lower grades. Buy Mint State 64 only in market pull backs for short-term profits. Buy Mint State 65 for longer hold periods. Proof 64 or better can be considered for larger portfolios.

**Three Dollar Gold Piece (1854–1889)**

A series with great untapped potential. Only two dates are readily available, 1854 and 1878, and these should be avoided. Many of the mintages range from 1,000 to 5,000 pieces.

If anyone ever realizes the potential of Three Dollar Gold Pieces, or if large sums of funds come into the rare coin market, this series could explode. Buy any you can afford in Mint State 63 or better. There is so much potential here in the mint state pieces that the higher priced proofs don't seem as attractive.

**Four Dollar Gold Piece (1879–1880)**

All are rare and struck in proof. A good long-term hold for the largest portfolios in Proof 63 or better.

**Half Eagle, Capped Bust to Right, Small Eagle (1795–1798)**

A beautiful coin but extremely rare in any condition, especially mint state.

## Half Eagle, Capped Bust to Right, Heraldic Eagle (1795–1807)

More modestly priced than the previous series but still beyond the reach of all but the largest portfolios.

## Half Eagle, Draped Bust Left (1807–1812)

Same comments apply as last series.

## Half Eagle, Capped Head to Left (1813–1834)

Best left to museums and large funds.

## Half Eagle, Classic Head (1834–1838)

Very scarce in mint state. We like this coin in Mint State 63 or better, but its price prohibits consideration for most portfolios. The crosslet 4 variety is very scarce and sometimes overlooked.

## Half Eagle, Liberty, No Motto (1839–1866)

Very scarce in mint state, but nobody seems to care. We like this coin in Mint State 63 or better but doubt its performance will live up to its rarity. Proof 63 or better should be considered.

## Half Eagle, Liberty, With Motto (1866–1908)

Common dates are a good short-term play in Mint State 64 during market pull backs. Mint State 65 is recommended for longer term. There are many scarce dates from several mints that could be profitable as longer holds in Mint State 64 or better. We like Proof 64 or better for long-term investment.

**Half Eagle, Indian (1908–1929)**

These coins are truly scarce in Mint State 64 or better. For the long term avoid the most common dates. Some lower population coins can be purchased at modest premiums above the common dates.

**Eagle, Capped Bust to Right, Small Eagle (1795–1797)**

A three year type coin with a total mintage of just over 13,000 pieces. Expensive in mint state but an excellent long-term hold.

**Eagle, Capped Bust to Right, Heraldic Eagle (1797–1804)**

Suitable for large holdings in Mint State 63 or better. The 1799 is the most common date. Avoid this if possible.

**Eagle, Liberty, No Motto (1838–1866)**

If you can find a Mint State 63 coin of this type it will perform very well. Truly scarce. Practically nonexistent in better grades.

### Eagle, Liberty, With Motto (1866–1907)

　　Due to the nature of the design of this coin any handling marks show easily. Even though millions were made, few have survived in Mint State 63 or better. Buy Mint State 63 on market pull backs. Buy Mint State 64 or better for the longer haul. Avoid the most common dates. Proof 64 or better is recommended if it fits your portfolio.

### Eagle, Indian, No Motto (1907–1908)

　　Overlooked as a type coin. The mintages, however, are low and very few survive in high quality. We like these in Mint State 64 or better.

## Eagle, Indian, With Motto (1908–1933)

A beautiful coin, very popular with investors and collectors alike. There are many very scarce dates. Recommended in Mint State 64 or better. Avoid the common dates.

## Double Eagle, Liberty, Type I (1849–1866)

Although the current supply of investment grade Type I pieces is very low we would recommend that you avoid this type. The possibility exists of a large infusion of pieces from salvaged treasure ships. Gold is practically inert and will continue to be retrieved from ships that went down in the Civil War era.

**Double Eagle, Liberty, Type II (1866–1876)**

Although this is not a popular coin, the highest quality mint state pieces and the few choice proofs available are excellent long-term holds.

**Double Eagle, Liberty, Type III (1877–1907)**

This is too lengthy a series and too expensive for date collectors to put much pressure on it, so consider it a type coin. Buy Mint State 64 on price dips and Mint State 65 for a long-term hold. Avoid the common 1904. Investors with large holdings can consider Proof 64 and better Twenty Dollar Liberties.

## Double Eagle, St. Gaudens, High Relief (1907)

One of the most beautiful coins every struck and extremely popular. Recommended in Mint State 64 or better. Readily available in lower grades—avoid these.

## Double Eagle, St. Gaudens, No Motto (1907–1908)

Because these coins were very softly struck they are quite unattractive versus the later "With Motto" issue. Avoid the 1908. Buy the 1908-D or 1907 in Mint State 64 or better.

**Double Eagle, St. Gaudens, With Motto (1908–1932)**

There is an abundant supply of these popular coins from Mint State 60 to 63. Don't buy them. Mint State 64 and 65 can be purchased during depressed markets to use as short-term plays. Key and semi-key dates are recommended for medium to long-term holds in Mint State 64 and better.

# COMMEMORATIVE SILVER COINS

There are 50 different types of silver commemorative coins: 48 halves, 1 quarter and 1 dollar. There are 144 total pieces counting varieties, dates, and mint marks.

Silver commemorative coins have been excellent investments over the years, but buying the correct pieces in the proper grade at the proper time is essential for success. These coins are very low mintage coins but were intended as collector pieces or souvenirs, so many have survived in mint state. Various coins of this series have been the subject of promotions at times. One should always examine the current price of a coin versus historic prices when following these recommendations.

### Isabella Quarter (1893)

The only silver commemorative quarter of the entire series and in demand by type collectors and collectors of the entire commemorative set. Recommended in Mint State 65 or better.

**Alabama Half Dollar, With 2x2 (1921)**

Entire mintage is only 6,006 pieces. Very difficult to find in high grade. Recommended in Mint State 65.

**Alabama Half Dollar, No 2x2 (1921)**

Although the mintage of this coin is much higher than the 2x2 variety it is equally difficult to find in Mint State 65 and is recommended.

**Albany Half Dollar (1936)**

Many high-quality pieces exist. Not currently recommended.

**Antietam Half Dollar (1937)**

These have survived in high quality with a moderate amount of Mint State 67 and Mint State 68 having been certified. Not currently recommended.

## Arkansas Half Dollar (1935–1939)

A total of 15 different date and mint mark combinations are available. Most survivors are not fully struck and are somewhat scuffy. Many pieces have mintages of just 2,000 to 5,000 coins, but we still don't like these coins because of their lack of eye appeal and lack of collector demand.

## Bay Bridge Half Dollar (1936-S)

There is a large hoard of these being held off the market and we don't recommend this coin.

## Boone Half Dollar (1934–1938)

Again, there is a large selection of dates and mint marks to fill the type collector's needs. There is a large supply of certified Mint State 65 and 66 and an ample amount of Mint State 67 coins. Not currently recommended.

## Bridgeport Half Dollar (1936)

The original mintage is a modest 25,000 pieces. Few survive above Mint State 65. The coin is recommended in Mint State 66.

**California Half Dollar (1925-S)**

Despite the high mintage (86,594 pieces) there are few survivors in Mint State 65 or better. A qualified recommendation in these grades. There is a hoard of Californias held off the market, but it is likely that the grades in this hoard will parallel those that are already available.

**Cincinnati Half Dollar (1936-P, D and S)**

A very popular set that fulfills the demand portion of the investment equation. The low original mintage is another positive signal for this series. Buy Mint State 65 and 66 coins. Avoid the Denver issue as it is much more available in higher grades.

## Cleveland Half Dollar (1936)

The price for this coin is relatively modest in Mint State 66 and is recommended for investment. Ideal for the investor with a low budget.

## Columbia Half Dollar (1936-P, D and S)

Although many of this low mintage coin have survived in high grade we like this coin in Mint State 67 because of its relatively modest price. Remember quality is extremely important to today's rare coin investors. It wouldn't take much buying pressure to cause the price of these coins to skyrocket.

### Columbian Exposition Half Dollar (1892–1893)

Our first commemorative half dollar and now very popular despite falling into disfavor for many years. A large portion of these coins found their way into circulation. We like both dates in Mint State 65 and better.

### Connecticut Half Dollar (1935)

This coin has a very beautiful design and is in demand by collectors and investors alike. The price level should be closely examined and compared to previous levels before investing. We feel the coin is often overpriced in Mint State 65 but quite reasonable in Mint State 66.

### Delaware Half Dollar (1936)

We like this coin in Mint State 66. The quantity available is modest and the demand is steady.

### Elgin Half Dollar (1936)

A good number survive in quality condition, but we like this coin in Mint State 66. Buy on market pull backs.

**Gettysburg Half Dollar (1936)**

Popular and attractive. Recommended in Mint State 66 and better.

**Grant Half Dollar, With Star (1922)**

The mintage is very low and few were made or survived in Mint State 65 quality, but everyone knows it. This coin is generally fully priced in Mint State 65 so it is not recommended.

## Grant Half Dollar, No Star (1922)

A large mintage by commemorative standards but not a large survival rate in Mint State 65 and higher. Recommended in Mint State 65 and 66.

## Hawaiian Half Dollar (1928)

Even the lowest grades of this coin are in demand by commemorative type collectors. The entry price is seldom cheap, but the mintage is low and few have survived in high grade. This is an excellent long-term hold. Recommended in Mint State 65.

## Hudson Half Dollar (1935)

Another low mintage coin. Tough to find in high grade. We recommend Mint State 66 coins to be purchased during lulls in the commemorative market.

## Huguenot Half Dollar (1924)

A large mintage for the series but most survivors are Mint State 64 or less. Recommended in Mint State 66.

## Illinois Half Dollar (1918)

This is another large mintage coin, a good portion of which is circulated or poorly stored uncirculated coins. There are, however, quite a few small hoards overhanging the market. Buy Mint State 67 when the entry price is reasonable.

## Iowa Half Dollar (1946)

The Iowa Centennial Commemorative Half Dollar is a high mintage coin with a very high number of survivors in Mint State 65, 66, and 67. On top of that, the state of Iowa is holding in bank vaults a large quantity of high-quality pieces for later release onto the marketplace. Avoid this coin.

### Lexington Half Dollar (1925)

This coin has always been tough to find in top condition. Recommended in Mint State 66.

### Long Island Half Dollar (1936)

Most of the mint state pieces are Mint State 64 or less. Recommended in Mint State 65 and better for investors who can keep an eye on the population of this high mintage coin.

## Lynchburg Half Dollar (1936)

Although not the most popular of coins and not among the most beautiful, only a modest number have survived in Mint State 66 or better and it is recommended in these grades.

## Maine Half Dollar (1920)

A large portion of this commemorative found its way into circulation. Also the majority of the mint state pieces are Mint State 64 or less. This coin is recommended in Mint State 65 and better, but only on price pull backs. At times it is fully priced.

## Maryland Half Dollar (1934)

This coin does not come fully struck and is rather unattractive. Not recommended.

## Missouri Half Dollar, 2x4 (1921)

Very scarce in Mint State and rare in investment quality. Usually not bargain priced. Buy on any price roll back and hold for long-term gain.

## Missouri Half Dollar, No 2x4 (1921)

The mintage of this variety is higher but in higher grades it is equally as scarce if not scarcer. Same advice as the 2x4. Buy on price roll backs.

## Monroe Half Dollar (1923-S)

A very high mintage compared to the series as a whole, but many pieces are circulated and very few are of investment quality. This date, unlike some other commemoratives, is usually fully priced. The money this will cost is better invested in some of the many underpriced coins in this series.

**New Rochelle Half Dollar (1938)**

These generally are available in fairly high quality but many just make Mint State 64 or 65. Invest in Mint State 66 or better, but keep one eye on the population report.

**Norfolk Half Dollar (1936)**

Many, many high-quality coins on the marketplace including some Mint State 68s, an easy opportunity to own a Mint State 67 or 68 coin. Buy the best you can afford on price roll backs.

## Oregon Half Dollar (1926–1939)

There are 14 different date and mint mark combinations of this very attractive and popular commemorative. The mintages for most are just 3,000 to 6,000 each. The big exceptions are the 1926 and 1926-S with mintages 5 to 15 times higher. We like the whole series, including the high mintage dates, and recommend it in the best grade you can afford. You or your dealer should carefully check current population and prices at the time you're considering investing. The 1933-D, over the years, has been strongly promoted. Buy this date when reasonable and sell into the promotions.

**Panama-Pacific Half Dollar (1915-S)**

   The number of high-quality pieces that have been certified is surprising versus how difficult it has been to locate them over the years. The prices are fairly strong also. We like this coin in Mint State 65 or better. Buy it on price corrections.

**Pilgrim Half Dollar (1920–1921)**

   Despite its high original mintage the 1920 Pilgrim has proven tough to acquire in high grades. Recommended in Mint State 66. The 1921 is tough to find in Mint State 66 and is recommended.

## Rhode Island Half Dollar (1936-P, D, and S)

These were not minted in the highest quality. Thus, there is a low population in quality grades. Recommended in Mint State 65 or better. The 1936-S seems particularly hard to find, but prices are equivalent for all dates.

## Roanoke Island Half Dollar (1937)

These are quite common in Mint State 65 and even 66. Recommend in Mint State 67 whenever the price is comparable to other 67s with similar population numbers.

## Robinson-Arkansas Half Dollar (1936)

Although there aren't large numbers in high grade, this coin is not popular or in great demand. There are better profit opportunities in other commemoratives.

## San Diego Half Dollar (1935-S, 1936-D)

The 1935 coin is quite available in high quality besides being hoarded. Avoid this one. You might try the 1936 in Mint State 66. It is possible that hoards of this date also exist.

## Sesquicentennial Half Dollar (1926)

Partly because of the method of manufacture (low-relief dies) and partly because of the high number that were placed in circulation, these coins are rare in investment quality. However, they are not a bargain in terms of price level, so avoid this issue.

## Spanish Trail Half Dollar (1935)

Very tough above Mint State 65 and recommended whenever the commemorative market is pulling back.

**Stone Mountain Half Dollar (1925)**

A huge mintage. Many, no doubt, have not been certified yet. Still, tough in better than Mint State 65. You might take a flyer on a Mint State 67 or 68. Otherwise avoid this issue.

**Texas Half Dollar (1934–1938)**

There are 13 different date and mint mark combinations for this series. The Texas commemoratives are one of the most popular and attractive designs of the commemorative series although some critics say the design is too cluttered. Most of the mintages are low to moderate ranging from 3,000 to 10,000 pieces. One exception is the 1934 with over 61,000 pieces. This is a highly promoted series and a case can be made for simply accumulating them during price lulls and selling them into promotions. There are also some legitimate bargains in the series including the high mintage 1934 in Mint State 66 or better. As a general recommendation invest in any Texas in Mint State 66 or better after comparing prices and population figures.

**Vancouver Half Dollar (1925)**

A hoard of 257 pieces came out in a 1982 auction, but most of these were not of gem quality. The populations of Mint State 65 and 66 are low. Recommended in these grades.

## Vermont Half Dollar (1927)

A large number of these commemoratives seem to have been mishandled and are hairlined or cleaned. Of the certified mint state pieces, the bulk of them are less than Mint State 65. Invest in Mint State 65 and better.

## Booker T. Washington Half Dollar (1946–1951)

Far too many pieces are available with 18 different date and mint mark combinations. This factor and a general lack of demand make this series a very poor investment.

## Washington Carver Half Dollar (1951–1954)

Twelve different date and mint mark combinations. Some high mintages and a lack of demand make this series another one to avoid. Although they are scarce in high quality, no one seems to care. Rarity is only a factor in coin investments when combined with demand.

## Wisconsin Half Dollar (1936)

The surviving population is far too high in Mint State 65 and 66. This one is recommended in Mint State 67 when price levels are favorable.

### York Half Dollar (1936)

The rims of this coin are the high points. Perhaps this explains the very high rate of surviving gem-quality pieces. Pass on this piece.

### Lafayette Dollar (1900)

Our only commemorative silver dollar excluding the rash of modern commemorative coinage. Most of the mintage has been circulated. Of the mint state pieces, few surpass Mint State 64. Still, not a recommendation for investment because it is usually fully priced. This coin can be considered in Mint State 64 or better on any large price drops.

# GOLD COMMEMORATIVE COINS

The commemorative gold series is made up of 13 different types, dates, and varieties, ranging in denomination from the one dollar pieces to the very rare $50 gold pieces. The mintages on most pieces are low and very few investment quality survivors are available.

## Grant Memorial Dollar, With Star (1922)

This is the most common of the gold commemoratives as far as investment quality survivors. Recommended in Mint State 66 when the commemorative market is down.

**Grant Memorial Dollar, No Star (1922)**

The Grant commemoratives are very popular. Demand combined with quality and scarcity make this a good investment in Mint State 65 and better, as long as the entry price is reasonable.

**Lewis and Clark Exposition Dollar (1904)**

The few available Mint State 65 pieces are recommended for investment whenever the prices for the gold commemorative series are depressed.

## Lewis and Clark Exposition Dollar (1905)

Very rare in Mint State 65 or better and usually fully priced. Invest in quality pieces only if bargain priced.

## Louisiana Purchase Jefferson Dollar (1903)

In comparison to the rest of the gold commemoratives this coin is one of the more common. Still, recommended in Mint State 65 or better.

## Louisiana Purchase McKinley Dollar (1903)

A little tougher than its companion piece above with the same recommendation.

## McKinley Memorial Dollar (1916)

A lot of these coins have either been mishandled or lightly circulated. Invest in Mint State 65 or better. Get in Mint State 66 if you can afford it.

## McKinley Memorial Dollar (1917)

The 1917 is much scarcer than the 1916 and this is reflected in the price. Recommended in Mint State 65 or better.

## Panama-Pacific Exposition Dollar (1915-S)

The population in Mint State 65 is modest, but we think it will continue to grow. Invest in Mint State 66 coins when prices are reasonable.

**Panama-Pacific Exposition Quarter Eagle (1915-S)**

This is a very tough coin to find in high quality and the population growth will probably be very small. Highly recommended in Mint State 65 or 66.

**United States Sesquicentennial Quarter Eagle (1926)**

This piece was overlooked for years because of its high mintage. Actually, relatively few Mint State 65 specimens have survived. It is, however, no longer a sleeper and seems fully priced. Pass this one up. There are better buys in the balance of the series.

**Panama-Pacific Exposition Fifty Dollar Round (1915-S)**

Obviously very rare and suitable only for the largest of portfolios. Buy Mint State 63 or better whenever reasonably priced in comparison to its price history.

**Panama-Pacific Exposition Fifty Dollar Octagonal (1915-S)**

The highlight of many auction sales along with the $50 Round. The Round is about of equal rarity in Mint State 63 or better and is recommended except in booming markets. Either piece is a good long-term hold.

# Glossary

**2x2, 2x4, etc.**

Several commemorative coins have a numeral, a star, and a second numeral somewhere in the field, indicating that Alabama, for example, was the twenty-second state of the Union, and Missouri the twenty-fourth.

**ADJUSTMENT MARKS**

Before the weights of coins became standardized in 1834, pieces that were weighed and found to be too heavy were filed down at the Mint. The areas where the coins were filed show abrasions that are known as "adjustment marks." They are frequently seen on early gold and silver coins. Such marks do not adversely affect value.

**ALLOY**

Mixture of more than one metal, usually preceded by the name of the most important metal in the mix; for example, "nickel alloy."

**ALTERED DATE (OR MINT MARK)**

The illegal practice of modifying a date or mint mark on a common coin to make it appear to be a rare coin.

**ANA**

Abbreviation for the American Numismatic Association.

**ANACS**

Abbreviation for the American Numismatic Association Certification Service.

## APPARENT WEAR
A coin may appear to have more wear than it actually has, due to poorly made dies or the prolonged use of worn dies.

## APPROVAL SALE
A retail or wholesale transaction in which the client inspects a coin delivered to him for a predetermined period of time before making a decision to buy.

## ARROWS (AT DATE)
During 1853–1885 and 1873–1874, arrowheads were placed to the left and right of the dates of certain varieties of half dollars, quarters, and dimes to indicate a change in the authorized weight of the coins.

## ASK
The price that a seller is willing to take in order to effect the sale of a coin.

## ATTRIBUTION
Identifying numismatic coins by such characteristics as date, mint, issuing authority, and the type of metal in which the item was struck.

## AUCTION
A method of selling; items are presented for sale to the highest bidder.

## AUTHENTICATION
Expert determination of the genuineness of a numismatic item.

## BAG
A $1,000 face-value bag of coins.

## BAG MARKS
The abrasions which coins receive through contact with one another. Most coins are thrown into bags soon after minting and shipped everywhere in the country. The coins bang against each other and usually receive a considerable number of abrasions. The presence of abrasions does not mean that a coin has been circulated, as all business strikes have some bag marks. Bag marks are a very important consideration in the grading of uncirculated coins.

## BID
The price that a dealer offers to pay for a coin.

## BIT
One-eighth of a Spanish milled dollar, equivalent in value to 12-1/2 cents. The term "two bits" comes from the use of this phrase in America

over a century ago.

**BLANK (OR BLANK PLANCHET)**

A piece of metal intended for coinage but not struck; see PLANCHET.

**BLUESHEET**

The *Certified Coin Dealer Newsletter*, a weekly report of Bid prices on certified (slabbed) coins; called the *Bluesheet* because it is printed with blue ink.

**BLUNDERED DIE**

A coinage die containing an error or "blunder" made by the die engraver—the punching of a date upside down, the misplacement of a letter, etc.

**BOILER ROOM**

A room where a group of fast-talking salespeople contact unsophisticated buyers in an effort to sell coins by telephone.

**BORDER**

Within the raised rim of a coin there was formerly a protective ornamentation either of radial lines or beads (see DENTICLES).

**BRANCH MINT**

Any United States Mint location other than Philadelphia. The first Branch Mints were established in the late 1830s in Charlotte (North Carolina), Dahlonega (Georgia), and New Orleans. Another formerly operated at Carson City (Nevada). Branch mints exist today in Denver, San Francisco, and West Point (see also MINT MARK).

**BRONZE**

An alloy composed of copper, zinc, and tin. Bronze has been used to produce U.S. coins since 1864, except for some years in which other alloys were employed.

**BU**

"Brilliant Uncirculated"; an abbreviation applied primarily to bags of coins to indicate that all coins in the bag are claimed to be Mint State.

**BULLION**

Precious metal in negotiable or tradable shape, such as a wafer, bar, or ingot.

**BULLION COIN**

A coin that has little numismatic value but is purchased for its precious metal content.

## BUSINESS STRIKE

A coin that is struck for commercial circulation purposes. Generally no special care is taken in the striking of such a coin as it is with a PROOF STRIKE.

## CABINET FRICTION

Slight surface wear on a coin caused by friction between it and the envelope or tray in which it was stored.

## CAMEO

Proof or proof-like coins with exceptional contrast between the fields and the devices. Generally there is a frosty appearance on the devices when set against mirror-like fields. Coins with strong cameo contrast usually sell at a premium.

## CARBON SPOT

A dark discoloration on the surface of a coin, caused either by a planchet imperfection prior to striking or by improper storage. If they are large enough, carbon spots can significantly lower the grade of a coin. They are most often found on copper coins.

## CERTIFIED

An adjective applied to any coin that has been examined by a professional numismatist and declared to be genuine. The term originated in reference to coins that were sent to ANACS and returned together with a "certificate." Now used to indicate any coin authenticated and perhaps graded by one of the recognized grading services.

## CHERRYPICK

Any process employed to obtain a rare date or die variety at the same price level as a common date or die variety. For example, purchasing bags of coins for the purpose of selecting or picking out the quality items that may be mixed with common date coins. Many specialized collectors use their knowledge to "cherrypick" coins from less informed dealers.

## CHOICE

An adjective used to describe especially select proof or uncirculated coins.

## CHOPMARK

A small punch mark or counterstamp applied to a coin, usually silver, by an oriental merchant through whose hands the coin passed; indicates that the merchant accepted the coin as genuine and of full weight and fineness. Chopmarks are frequently found on U.S. Trade Dollars of the 1873–1878 era.

**CIRCULATED**

A coin passed from hand to hand in commerce and, in the process, becoming smoothed or worn; a used coin.

**CLAD**

A coin composed of layered metals. For example, a silver clad or copper-nickel clad U.S. coin dated from 1965 to the present.

**CLASH MARKS**

Marks appearing on the surface of a coin that was struck with a die that previously had been struck by another die with no planchet between them. These are common on 19th-century coins and do not adversely affect value.

**CLASSIC HEAD DESIGN**

A standardized motif used on various U.S. coin issues, primarily in the early 19th century; one example is the Large Cents of 1808–1814; a variety of the LIBERTY HEAD.

**CLIPPED PLANCHET**

When a coin is improperly ejected and as a result has a segment "clipped" from its edge. Of interest primarily to mint error collectors.

**COINING DIE**

See WORKING DIE.

**COLLAR**

A mechanism that is used to keep the dies in place during the time of striking so that the planchets do not move around.

**COMMEMORATIVES**

Coins that have been issued by the U.S. government to celebrate important events in the history of the country. These coins are extremely popular with collectors.

**COMMON DATE**

Coins with dates that are easy to acquire, usually because they were originally minted in large quantities. See also KEY DATE.

**CONDITION**

The diagnostic features that describe a coin's state of preservation.

**CONDITION CENSUS**

A term invented by Dr. William H. Sheldon to encompass the average condition of the five finest-known specimens of a given variety of large cents; used today by some catalogers with other series.

**CONDITION RARITY**

Of the known specimens of a coin, the relatively few that are exceptionally rare and, thus, in investment (generally, uncirculated or proof) condition.

**CONTACT MARKS**

See **BAG MARKS**.

**COPY**

See **REPRODUCTION.**

**CORROSION**

Damage that occurs on the surface of some coins, generally due to improper storage. Corrosion is caused when a chemical reaction, such as rust, actually eats into the metal.

**COUNTERFEIT**

Not genuine; a FAKE.

**DATE**

The numerals on a coin that specify the year it was struck.

**DEFECTIVE DIE**

Coins that show raised metal from a large die crack or a small rim break.

**DENTICLES**

The toothlike projections or design ornamentations located on the inner rim of some coins. These were discontinued on most U.S. coins in the early 20th century.

**DESIGNER**

The creator of a coin design; for example, Augustus St. Gaudens designed the $20 gold coin that bears his name.

**DEVICE**

The principle design elements of a coin, which appear as raised, or incused, areas and serve as the focal points of the artist's design. Typically, the reverse device is represented by an eagle and the obverse device, perhaps, the head of "Liberty."

**DIE**

The engraved punch used to strike coins.

**DIE BREAK** or **DIE CRACK**

Raised lines on the surface of a coin as a result of that coin having been struck by a broken or cracked die.

## DIE ENGRAVER'S LINES

Raised lines appearing on the surface of a coin that are the result of tool markings placed on the die during the design process by a Mint engraver.

## DIE VARIETY

A coin that has different characteristics from all other pieces struck the same year from other dies. Usually refers to coins which exhibit unusual characteristics that make them noticeably different from their contemporaries.

## DIE WEAR

The loss of detail on a coin due to wear on the dies used to strike it rather than wear from circulation of the coin.

## DIME

U.S. 10-cent piece; one tenth of a dollar.

## DIPPED

A coin that has had its natural toning removed by placing it in a mildly acidic or alkaline solution. Dipping will cause noticeable dulling of luster, especially on copper coins.

## DISK

See PLANCHET.

## DISME

Early spelling of the word "dime"; used for pattern issues of 1792; later the silent "s" was dropped.

## DOUBLE DIE

An error in die preparation caused by a working die receiving one blow from the hub (which is used to make the coining dies) and then a second, slightly misaligned, blow from the hub die. The result is coins that are blurred and display a slight doubling of the image. An example is the 1955 Double Die Cent.

## DOUBLE EAGLE

A U.S. gold coin with a face value of $20; see EAGLE.

## DRAPED-BUST DESIGN

Design for U.S. coinage of several denominations during the late 17th and 18th centuries.

## EAGLE

A U.S. gold coin having a face value of $10. The standard from which all other early U.S. gold coins derive their value, either in fractions or in multiples of an Eagle.

**ERROR**

A mistake in the manufacture of a coin.

**EYE APPEAL**

The aesthetic effect that a coin has on its viewer. Although somewhat subjective, coins that have (or do not have) eye appeal are generally agreed upon by most experienced numismatists.

**FAKE**

A coin that has been either reproduced illegally or modified in some way so as to make appear to be a genuine rare coin; a forgery.

**FIAT MONEY**

The name formerly given to paper money that was issued by a government but which was not redeemable in coin or bullion.

**FIELD**

The flat, open areas of a coin's design that surround the devices and other raised portions of the surface. Visually important to most numismatists when grading a coin.

**FIRST STRIKE**

Early impression from working dies that still have their initial polishing. See PROOF-LIKE.

**FLIP**

A clear, flexible plastic holder used to display and store raw coins.

**FLOP**

The practice of trading at the wholesale level between dealers for 2% to 5% profit.

**FLOWING-HAIR DESIGN**

An early design used on U.S. coins.

**FLYSPECKS**

Tiny surface discolorations found on copper, copper-nickel, and nickel coins.

**FROSTY**

An adjective used to describe a coin or some portion of a coin that possesses intense luster that is not mirrorlike. Devices of cameo-proof coins are considered frosty.

**GEM**

An adjective commonly used by numismatists to describe a coin that they would grade as MS-65 or Proof-65 or higher.

## GENERIC COINS

Coins that within a specific issue are considered to be "common" or easily obtainable (and thus less expensive) in that date and grade than in the more rare dates and higher grades; type coins with the lowest bids.

## GRADE

A shorthand term to convey the condition or state of preservation of a coin. One of the main determinants of coin value. May be expressed numerically (from 1 to 70), with words ("Good," "Fine," "Almost Uncirculated"), or by a combination of the two ("MS-65"). See SHELDON SCALE.

## GREYSHEET

*The Coin Dealer Newsletter*, a weekly periodical that lists approximate dealer Bid and Ask coin prices. Nicknamed the *Greysheet* because it is printed on grey paper.

## HALF EAGLE

A United States $5 Gold Piece; see EAGLE.

## HAIRLINES

Tiny scratches on a coin, caused by cleaning or wiping it with a cloth. Always considered to be distracting; when they appear in significant quantities on a proof, the coin may be called "impaired."

## HIGH RELIEF

A coin with deep concave fields due to its design. High-relief coins require extra pressure to be fully struck and are difficult to stack. Because of this, the few coins struck in high relief by the U.S. Mint (for example, the 1921 Peace Dollar and the 1907 Roman Numeral Double Eagle) were each made for one year only.

## HUB or HUB DIE

A piece of steel containing a coin's design; used to produce Working Dies. See also DOUBLE DIE.

## IMPAIRED PROOF

A proof coin that has numerous hairlines or has been mishandled or abused.

## INCUSE(D)

Designs recessed below the surrounding surface rather than raised above it; intaglio, the opposite of bas relief. Gold Indian Quarter Eagles and Half Eagles (1908–1929) are the only U.S. coins with an incused design.

**IRIDESCENT**

A desirable toning on a silver or nickel coin. Iridescent toning covers virtually all of the coin's surface, while still permitting all of the coin's natural luster to shine through with its full intensity. Some numismatists feel that in order for toning to be called iridescent, it must have all or most of the colors of the rainbow.

**KEY DATE**

A specific coin date that, within a series as a whole, commands a strong premium for its rarity. The opposite of COMMON DATE.

**LEGEND**

"United States of America" inscribed on a coin.

**LETTERED EDGE**

A coin produced with an inscription around the edge.

**LIBERTY**

Name given to the allegorical feminine portrait or figure on many U.S. coins; sometimes called "Miss Liberty."

**LIBERTY-CAP DESIGN**

The Liberty Cap, a headpiece given to slaves in ancient times when they secured their freedom, was symbolic of America as a free country. The Liberty Cap appears as part of many U.S. coin designs.

**LINT MARK**

A characteristic that occurs mostly on proof coins as a result of a piece of lint on the die or planchet during the striking process. This lint creates an incused, scratchlike mark on the coin. Lint marks are wider, deeper, and more visible than hairlines. They are also identifiable by their interesting threadlike shapes. Since a lint mark is mint-caused, it has a much smaller effect on the value of a coin than a hairline of equal size and prominence.

**LUSTER**

The sheen, brightness, or brilliance of a coin's surface caused by metal flowing toward the edge as it is being struck. Generally there are three types of luster: satiny, frosty, and Proof-like. The various consistencies of luster are predicated on how the dies were polished before striking, the quality of the planchets used, and the overall methodology of strike.

**MASTER DIE**

The die used to produce several Hub Dies, which in turn are used to make the Working Dies. The Master Die may be used, for example, to produce Hub Dies that are then sent to different mints, where the dates and mint marks are added before making the Working Dies. The Master Die is never used to strike coins.

## MATTE PROOF

A proof coin with finely granulated surfaces, officially produced by the issuing authority. Matte proof coins were minted by the U.S. mostly around and just following the beginning of the 20th century.

## MILLED EDGE

A coin with a rim around the edge.

## MILLING MARK

A series of two or more small nicks on a coin that result from contact with the reeded edge of another coin.

## MINT

Any facility where coins are struck or manufactured.

## MINT MARK

An identifying mark, usually a small letter, to indicate the city where the Branch Mint that produced the coin is located.

## MINT RED

The original reddish coloration found on copper coinage.

## MIRROR LIKE

See CAMEO.

## MOTTO

Inscription on coin reading "In God We Trust."

## MULING

An intentional or unintentional striking that mates one die with another it was not supposed to be mated with.

## OBVERSE

The front side of a coin; "heads."

## ORIGINAL BAG

A sack of uncirculated coins, all of the same date, that were assembled at the time of manufacture at a mint. For example, a sack containing 1,000 silver dollars, all minted at the same time and at one location.

## ORIGINAL ROLL

A roll of coins that have been together since the time of issue and in which most or all are uniform in appearance and quality.

## OVERDATE
A coin on which one or more of the original digits in the date has been punched a second time with another numeral, leaving the numeral underneath visible below the overpunch.

## OVERSTRIKE
A coin that is passed through the dies a second time, either by error or for the purpose of preparing an exceptionally strong design imprint. Proof coins are regularly struck more than once.

## PAPERED
A coin that has been certified as to authenticity and/or grade by providing the owner with a paper certificate; usually refers to coins certified by the American Numismatic Association Certification Services (ANACS).

## PATTERN
A design prototype; an experimental striking, perhaps in a metal other than that which will ultimately be used, for the purpose of considering the coin as a potential regular issue.

## PEDIGREE
The sales history of a particular coin or set.

## PERIPHERY
The inner border of a coin, usually encompassing the stars on the obverse and the legend on the reverse.

## PLANCHET
The circular blank piece of metal from which a coin is struck; also called a "Blank" or a "Disk."

## PLANCHET FLAW
A mint-made flaw on the surface of a coin that is the result of improper alloying or annealing of the planchet.

## POROSITY
Mint-made or non-mint-made roughness on a coin that goes into the surface.

## PRESENTATION PIECES
Coins minted with unusual care from new dies on carefully selected blanks; intended as gifts for "VIPs" on visits to the mint.

## PRIVATE TREATY
A transaction occurring between coin dealers handled by telephone or in person that bypasses the electronic coin trading exchanges.

## PROOF

A coin struck, usually with two or more blows from highly polished dies, and using specially prepared planchets. This process produces coins that have mirror-like surfaces. Proof is not a grade but a method of manufacture. Proof coins are made for collectors and not for general circulation.

## PROOF-LIKE

An uncirculated, business strike that has a partial mirror-like surface, the result of having been struck from polished dies but not specially struck as a proof.

## PROOF SET

A set consisting of one proof coin of each denomination issued by a particular mint during a specific year.

## PROTECTED AREAS

The parts of the fields of a coin that are nearest to the devices, legends, or the date. On lightly worn coins, the remaining luster is often confined to the protected areas.

## PVC

Polyvinyl chloride. The chemical material many flips are made of. Over extended periods of time this chemical material will produce a residue that will turn the surfaces of coins green.

## QUARTER EAGLE

A United States $2-1/2 Gold Piece; see EAGLE.

## RARE

A comparative term denoting a high degree of scarcity.

## RAW

Any coin that has not been authenticated and graded by one of services and placed in a tamper-proof, plastic slab; see also SLABBED.

## RED BOOK

*A Guide Book of United States Coins* by R.S. Yeoman. Published annually (the 1990 edition is the 43rd revision), this book gives the original mintage figures and illustrated descriptions of almost all U.S. coins and coin variations.

## REEDED EDGE

Raised parallel lines on the outside edge of the coin.

## REPRODUCTION

A copy so marked, as required by law, with an "R" or a "C."

**RESTRIKE**

A coin struck after the date that appears on the coin.

**REVERSE**

The back side of a coin; "tails."

**RIM BUMP** or **RIM NICK**

A depression on the edge of a coin, often caused by its having been dropped against a hard surface or through contact with another coin, as in a bag of coins.

**RIP**

An especially fortuitous coin purchase, made by either a collector or a dealer.

**ROLL**

Original coins, assembled at the time of manufacture, usually by a bank, and then placed into a standard-sized paper tube. There are, for example, 20 dollars in a roll.

**SLABBED**

A coin that has been authenticated and graded by one of the recognized services and sealed in a tamper-proof plastic container or "slab"; see also RAW.

**SLEEPER**

A coin that is regarded as being underrated, undervalued, or overlooked in comparison with other more highly priced issues.

**SLIDER**

A coin that is slightly below but very close to the grade indicated. The term usually refers to a nearly Mint State coin which is, or could be offered as, full Mint State.

**SPLIT GRADE**

A coin that grades differently on one side than on the other.

**STRONG**

A coin exhibiting exceptional detail, usually in a particular area.

**TONING**

Patination or natural coloration that is caused by chemical reaction over a period of time between airborne elements such as sodium and the coinage metal. Attractive toning can add considerable value to a coin.

**TRANSITIONAL**

A coin which mates the die of one particular type or design with another that was not adopted until a later date. This mating may be intentional or unintentional.

**TYPE**

A classification of coins by distinguishable design changes. The word "type" is capitalized when identifying coins because it refers to a specific category of collectible coin, a major variety. For example, the Draped Bust Dime with Small Eagle on the reverse is considered a coin type even though it was minted for only two years. On the other hand, the Barber Dime is a coin type that was minted from 1892 to 1916. Appendix B lists almost every U.S. coin type.

**TYPE COIN**

A coin that has no significant commonality or rarity premium within its specific series. It is thus chosen by the "type collector" as being "typical" of that series.

**TYPE SET**

A set of type coins that share specific characteristics. For example, an American Gold Type Set would include one example of each type of gold coin issued by the U.S. Mint from 1795 to 1933. See also VARIETY.

**UNC**

"Uncirculated"; a coin that does not exhibit the normal wear that comes from changing hands many times in commercial transactions.

**VARIETY**

A classification of coins characterized only by a visible change in the die as opposed to a TYPE, which is characterized by a change in the design.

**VERDIGRIS**

Removable green spots found on the surface of a coin that are the result of a chemical reaction between airborne contaminants and the coinage metal.

**WEAK**

A coin exhibiting weak detail in a particular area. See also STRONG.

**WHIZZING**

Any process such as buffing, burnishing, polishing, wire brushing, or acid treatment, that is designed to make a coin look better than it actually is. Most whizzed coins have an unnaturally shiny appearance due to abrasive action. Coins are also whizzed to remove or reduce unsightly abrasions or to mask the effects of adding or removing a mint mark or altering a date. Any process like this destroys the coin's natural surface and is considered extremely detracting.

## WIRE EDGE

A coin with a sharp, knife-like rim.

## WIRE RIMS

When excess metal is squeezed into the collar that surrounds the dies, this metal has nowhere to go. Thus, it is extruded up and down, producing a wire rim. Wire rims are most frequently found on proof coins.

## WORKING DIE

Any die that is actually used to produce coins; the product of a HUB DIE.

# Index

# C

Carmichael, Hoagie  1
Caruso, Enrico  1
*CCDn Asksheet*  66
CCE
    *see* Certified Coin Exchange
certificates of deposit  7
*Certified Coin Dealer Newsletter*  64, 66
Certified Coin Exchange (CCE)  31, 36, 42, 44, 45, 61, 62, 64, 65, 66, 77, 80
Chagall  56
Chamber of Commerce  35
CNAC
    *see* Consumer Numismatic Advisory Commission
*Coin Dealer Newsletter*  6, 64
*Coin World*  64
collateral  7
    coins as  9
collectibles  6
Commodity Futures Trading Commission (CFTC)  9
Consumer Numismatic Advisory Commission (CNAC)  69, 79, 81, 82
Consumer Price Index (CPI)  2, 4

# D

demand  7, 8
diminishing supply  7
Double Eagle  52
downside risk, limited  8
Draped Bust  73

# E

Ebsen, Buddy  1

# F

Farouk, King  1, 13
Federal Reserve  52
Federal Trade Commission (FTC)  41

# G

General Electric  12, 18, 21, 86
gold ownership, legalized  53
Gold Surrender Order of 1933  51, 52
grading services  25

# BIOGRAPHICAL SKETCHES

MICHAEL L. YERGIN appears on national TV and radio and conducts seminars on numismatics throughout the United States. Mr. Yergin has an extensive background in numismatics, real estate, and many other investments and is Chairman of one of the leading numismatic companies in North America. Mr. Yergin is a member of the American Numismatic Association in Colorado Springs, Colorado, and the Industry Council for Tangible Assets in Washington, DC, and is the honorary Chairman of the Consumer Numismatic Advisory Commission in Washington, DC. Mr. Yergin is also listed in the 27th edition of *Who's Who in Finance and Industry in America*. In addition to being a well-known radio personality, he still finds time to be active in politics, charitable causes, and helping the underprivileged.

LAURA A. GRAVES is a well-known lecturer, author, and coin expert and is the President of a leading numismatic company. Ms. Graves is a member of the Industry Council for Tangible Assets and is known throughout the numismatic community as a storehouse of knowledge on numismatics, with her field of expertise being U.S. gold and silver rare coins. Ms. Graves is Research Director for *COINews*, a highly respected monthly numismatic publication. Ms. Graves, in addition to caring for her family, supports many political and charitable causes.

DR. ROBERT G. CHENHALL, besides being an acutely knowledgeable coin collector/investor, has written and published over 50 articles and five books. Dr. Chenhall is a CPA and has worked for Price Waterhouse, Del Webb Corporation, and as a licensed stockbroker. He is a principal in a very successful leasing company. Dr. Chenhall has extensive knowledge in a variety of fields ranging from rare coins and finance to archeology. He has been director of various museums, a college professor, lecturer, and has an impressive numismatic collection. Dr. Chenhall is listed in *Who's Who in America*.